# The Jumble Sale Handbook

### An In-depth Exposé from Both Sides of the Trestle

by Frances Pitt

with cartoons by Colin Whittock

## CENTURY

LONDON  SYDNEY  AUCKLAND  JOHANNESBURG

By the same author

*The Chronological Atlas of World War II*
(with Barrie Pitt)

First published in 1991 by Century
Random Century Ltd
20 Vauxhall Bridge Road, London SW1V 2SA

Random Century Australia (Pty) Ltd
20 Alfred Street, Milsons Point,
Sydney, NSW 2061, Australia

Random Century New Zealand Ltd
18 Poland Road, Glenfield,
Auckland 10, New Zealand

Random Century South Africa (Pty) Ltd
PO Box 337, Bergvlei 2012, South Africa

The right of Frances Pitt to be identified as the author of this work has been asserted by her in accordance with the Copyright, Designs and Patents Act, 1988.

Set in Linotron Plantin

Printed and bound in Great Britain

British Library Cataloguing in Publication Data
Pitt, Frances
    The jumble sale handbook.
    1. Jumble sales. Attending
    I. Title
    658.8703

ISBN 0-7126-4660-4

# Contents

*To all my friends in the queue
and foes in the Great Rush,
especially
Eve, Hilda, London Stan, Sylvia,
Jack and Angie, Ken, Joyce
and Julie, Cliff and Maureen,
Lady Martita and the wife of
my consultant gynaecologist.*

# Introduction

According to the autobiographical note in the front of all Dick Francis' novels, I think that my relationship to jumble sales must be rather like his to riding. He can't remember learning to ride; I can't remember first going to a jumble.

But I do remember the atmosphere of those early jumble sales, held on Saturday afternoons from autumn to spring. We lived in Highbury, London, and jumbling became indelibly linked in my young mind with roars of triumph or disaster emanating from the Arsenal Football Ground just along the road. Even on the dullest and greyest day an air of excitement enlivened the whole area, and although it can't have occurred invariably, it still seems to me that the flinging open of the church hall doors and the surge of the Great Rush (see Glossary) was always accompanied by the deep, drum-like echo of forty thousand voices bouncing off a stadium canopy. It was many years before I actually *saw* a football match, and then on telly – but it struck me when I did that the game which had produced that roar of the crowd was tame compared to the fire and fury of what would always be to me the real thing, the jumble sale; and not half as satisfying.

In those days I was taken to sales by my Aunt Molly, much to the disapproval of my mother, who was very particular and thought I might catch something nasty whilst indulging in such a *common* pursuit – but I brought back nothing worse than the odd knocked-about toy, bought with my pocket money thrupenny bit, and all the more cherished by me for that. Later, my family moved to a New Town, thirty miles north of London, and, once I was parted from my dear and enthusiastic aunt, jumble sales faded from my life. But their influence remained, for every so often the family took the train up to town – my mother, father, sister and myself with a large empty suitcase – and we called on Aunt Molly at the terraced flat where she lived with my uncle and cousin. After the gossip had been exchanged, mother, sister and I were shepherded into the big bedroom, gloomy with too many pieces of heavy Victorian furniture, but where we spent a blissful afternoon trying on all the wonderful clothes Molly had grabbed for us from jumble sales in Hampstead, Knightsbridge and Kensington; she even occasionally intimated that some of them came from Royalty, which impressed mother no end! On the way home in the train, with our new wardrobes carefully folded in the suitcase on the rack, we were reminded yet again that if anyone asked where our clothes came from, we were to say they were 'Molly Modes', a small vanity of my mother's that we children thought amusing and so readily complied.

During my teens I was stirred once or twice to consider going jumbling; I remember most particularly Barbara of the flaming red hair boasting of her gorgeous fur coat bargain that had cost her one shilling and sixpence – I wanted to scratch her eyes out; but each time, another party or date with a new boyfriend took my attention and the moment passed. I developed a career, a husband; then came children and, although I occasionally saw advertisements for jumble sales, I knew my spouse wouldn't like me to attend – it wouldn't look good in the eyes of the neighbours – and as there was no Saturday football crowd roar to act subliminally I didn't mind following his wishes.

However, we fell out about other things, so I eventually acquired a new husband, and a village home where I was keen to settle and become one of the locals. Helping with fundraising in the area was one way of joining in, but I resisted the jumble sales that seemed to occur weekly . . . until one Saturday lunchtime, when I found my new beloved, Carlsberg Special Brew in hand, muscles taut, eyes like saucers, in a darkened living room, shouting at the television screen; it was the start of the rugby season. The roar of the crowd battered me as I walked in; and so did the spectacle! It all came back! International rugby indeed reminded me of old times – the shoving, the protruding elbows, the swing of powerful hips to block a competitor for a choice bargain . . . er, oval ball . . . the quick tucking of the spoils under the arm and the rapid scuttle away towards home and triumph. It was obvious that my man really believed he was playing the game, as he lunged forward to parry a ball aimed at the camera or leapt upright to grab thin air, and I was fired by the same feeling, which in my case became a strong conviction that I should go jumbling. I tip-toed out of the room, for hadn't I seen a sale advertised for three o'clock?

With considerable trepidation I set out, and was amazed at the number of people already waiting in the queue when I tacked myself onto the end. In the few minutes I had to wait before opening time, I recognised the doctor's wife, my snooty next-door neighbour and the lady from the manor house, as well as a lot of clean, well-dressed people who didn't look in great need of charity; but then the Great Rush caught me up and swirled me in through the hall doors, and I really remembered little of the next minutes – or hours – until I arrived home, made a cup of tea (which, God knows, I needed) and surveyed my catch.

I'd got no further than pulling out the top item from the first of the stuffed carrier-bags (a gruesome, mustard-coloured blouse) and was wondering what on earth had possessed me to buy it, when I heard the tread of my husband as he crossed the hall and was torn between an overwhelming desire to tell him all about it and panic. He wouldn't like it; more, he would *hate* it that I'd been to a jumble sale. In the end my exhilaration was such that there was no way I could keep quiet and as he came through the door I cast myself into his arms, babbling about it being all right really because the doctor's wife was there and if she could go, why couldn't I? And when he sees the bargains I've brought home and . . . he laughed and gazed fondly at me, recognising that I was on the same sort of 'high' that he had just experienced from that good game of rugby and was delighted to see me so animated. I began pulling my bargains from their bags: nothing really special by my standards of today, but to us both, that first time, each one was a little gem. There were a couple of lambswool jumpers (later discarded as too itchy), a skirt or two, trousers and T-shirts for my children to wear for play, a good school pullover for the boy and a pretty nightie for the girl, six attractive plates, a very nice striped tie . . . and the bilious yellow blouse. As I flourished each before his eyes, begging his approbation and quoting how much – or how little – I had paid for it, his eyebrows almost disappeared up under his hair, and he shot me what my mother would have called 'old-fashioned looks'. I was eager to reassure him that I'd done nothing to increase the overdraft and when I emptied my purse to show I was still in possession of the greater part of the week's housekeeping money he was, indeed, convinced. And when we both realised that the plates were good bone china and the tie real silk, I knew I was hooked; that on future Saturdays he would caper round the living room, I would caper round various village halls and we would meet for tea afterwards, both of us with stars in our eyes!

I went to the next sale; it was an anticlimax. It rained, the queue was affected and disinclined to chat amongst themselves, let alone with me; and the tables were set out in an unsystematic way that confused me – and, from overheard comments, other people too. I came away thinking the pound or so I'd handed over the trestles had not been particularly well spent. On my arrival home the whole family met in the kitchen. My husband had 'played' a disappointing game (he was on the wrong side, that week) and I sought to mollify him with a couple of rather tatty Wodehouse paperbacks, which did the trick as he had read neither of them and they were both long out of print; my daughter pounced with delight upon a black dress I'd mistakenly bought for myself, not realising it was three sizes too small for me, and my son adopted an unusual tumbler as his own, special drinking glass. And weighing down the bottom of the bag was an object that I'd picked up to look at, and was so cross when someone tried eagerly to snatch it from me that I'd spent twenty pence on it without knowing what it was. It seemed to be a flat metal oblong, about five centimetres long, two and a half wide and one thick, with one end hinged to open. It was almost black with age and discoloration, and when I found out a day or so later that it was in fact a very old match case – a Vesta case, someone told me – I wasn't very excited. It could always go back on the White Elephant stall, but I might as well clean it. So I did, and it looked very nice; and I looked at the hallmark through a magnifying glass. Solid silver . . . for twenty pence! I wasn't just hooked – I was *harpooned*!!!

It wrought something of a change in my life, as you can imagine. No longer could invitations for Saturday lunch-time drinks be lightly accepted, and instead of idly glancing through the local paper some time during the weekend, now on a Friday morning I am lying in wait to snatch the paper from the newsboy's hands. Then follows the plotting. Times are juggled, approach and escape routes are carefully worked out, and especially cross-town routes to take me rapidly from one event to another, preferably on foot in order to avoid wasting time parking. Over the years I have learnt the value of careful appraisal, not only of the probable quality of goods in each sale, judged not least by the group holding it and the area it is in, but by personal experience and that of other jumblers of whether the atmosphere in the hall will be pleasant or hostile, the prices high or low. And I regard reconnaissance of the locale, should it be an unfamiliar one, as essential. My husband tells me that Field Marshal Montgomery took a similar view.

Meals and family need organisation and instruction, of course – and some training helps in the end. The children can become participants. My daughter, Carrie, proved a particularly apt pupil and through her teens has been able to stun her friends with the sheer quantity of different 'amazing', 'ace' and 'brill' clothes she possesses. Her imaginative alterations – tie-dying them in grim colours, slashing, drastic shortening – perturb me not one jot when the whole lot cost less than a fiver! And my dear husband has become skilled at maintaining a show of interest in the inevitable fashion parade that always follows a jumbling session, even when it's out of the rugby season. The secret was to bring him something exceptional – which in my case was an immaculate Pierre Cardin double-breasted blazer that cost twenty-five pence and needed only a new shoulder pad to make him look as though he'd been especially designed to fit into it.

Since then he has been at least interested, and at best eager, to examine my haul and listen to my narratives; and it was as a result of hearing my comments and criticisms of the day's jumbling that he enquired one afternoon if there existed such a thing as an instruction manual for jumble sales! It wasn't long, of course, before my interest became apparent to others and I found myself engaged by local fundraisers as a sort of consultant in all the stages intrinsic to the operation – from first committee meeting to clearing up afterwards. I felt it incumbent upon me to give my very best effort and raked together all the stories of thieves, rogues and just plain cheeky devils that I had encountered, all the silly mistakes I had seen other organisers make and some of their clever innovations, to recount to my incredulous fellow helpers, who seemed to enjoy them, as we set about arranging the sale. I began to think of my husband's suggestion of a handbook as a possiblity; and someone like me, who had seen it all, ought to write it. This book is the result.

The setting-up and running of a jumble sale is undoubtedly an activity as full of triumph, disaster, exultation and despair as any other form of advanced human endeavour; and, from the time of first conception to exhausting finale, can wring the soul. All human life, if I am not infringing a copyright, is there. It is difficult for me to decide which aspect satisfies me most – sorting through the goods before they go on sale and the fun of helping, or sorting through what I have brought home from someone else's sale. Both can be sources of high excitement.

There are also friends to be made. Eve is eighty-four, lives by herself, has a bad heart yet walks miles weighed down by bags of jumble she has bought on the other side of town. She makes a lovely cup of tea and gives me one whenever I drive her home, and we have a good long natter about past conflicts and triumphs won. And I have waved companionably (during a working lunch) to another jumble-bug across the floor of Claridge's dining room, and nobly kept secret from my host where the lady's superbly cut skirt had come from, and what it cost (fifty pence – she beat me to it by a split fingernail). On the other hand, I might have enjoyed the look on my host's face had I told him my whole outfit (except for expensive shoes and perfume) cost less than the tip he'd given the cocktail waiter! It's a great life.

But of all the appealing aspects, the truly inspirational moment is the same – that breathless interval just before the doors are flung open and the Great Rush is launched,

When Expectation hangs in the Air

And all the Heavens

CRY HAVOC!

And let slip the Bugs of Jumble Sale.

## Author's Note

I should like to thank the many people who helped in the compilation of this book – not least the dozens of jumblers who told me their tales as we whiled away hours of queuing. My gratitude goes also to officials of the Department of Health, particularly Dr Billingham, Ms Gitter and Mr McGovern; the Trading Standards Offices of both Yeovil and Taunton, with special thanks to Mr Fowler; and to various officers of Taunton Deane Borough and Somerset County Councils, notably Mr Swift. Valuable information was furnished by Mr Ellis of the Commercial Union and Mr Lawford of Key Management Insurance Services, while Mrs Zoers of the Community Council for Somerset gave much needed support. Likewise ACRE, Action with Communities in Rural England, Cirencester, came to my assistance with their Village Halls Information sheet. Sally Capper's *But is it Legal?* (Bedford Square Press, 1988) proved a mine of information, as did *The Woman's Own Book of Fundraising* (Collins, 1988).

Terms for the Glossary were checked in the *Oxford English Dictionary*, whilst the history chapter owes a great deal to *A History of Shopping* by Dorothy Davis (Routledge & Kegan Paul, 1966), *England in the Age of Hogarth* by Derek Jarrett (Yale University Press, 1986), *Life in Shakespeare's England* compiled by John Dover Wilson (Penguin Shakespeare Library, 1968), *Landlords to London* by Simon Jenkins (Constable, 1975) and the *Encyclopaedia Britannica*.

Further thanks are due to my typist, Sally-Ann Halstead, and, most importantly, to Barrie Pitt for his patient reading and re-reading of the typescript, his advice and support, and his time given so generously whenever I interrupted work on his current book.

# *Glossary*

Any interest fervently pursued by a lot of people engenders its own vocabulary; the jumble sale is no exception.

**Jumble sale**
A term that first came to the notice of the *Oxford English Dictionary* in 1931 as a charitable sale of mostly second-hand goods, but was probably in use before that to describe any mixed-up mass of goods for sale. May be shortened to 'jumble' without the 'sale'.

**Rummage sale**
The same as jumble sale; the term is preferred in some areas of Great Britain and in the United States. Rummage originally referred to the arrangement of casks in a ship's hold and from this the rummage sale evolved in the nineteenth century as a sale of unclaimed goods in a warehouse or on a wharf.

**To jumble**
It is fortunate indeed that the sixteenth-century meaning of this verb doesn't rush readily to mind, for some people may be a little put out to find they have announced they are about to 'have carnal knowledge of' when all they intend doing is 'attend as a customer one or more jumble sales'.

**Jumble-bug**
Someone with a passionate love of jumble sales which may include helping at, as well as attending, them.

**Jumblophile**
An intellectual jumble-bug.

**Jumblophobe**
Someone whose flesh crawls at the thought of second-hand clothes and who has a very low opinion of jumblophiles.

**Jumbler**
This is someone whose weekend is not necessarily ruined by withdrawal symptoms if no sales are advertised in the local paper, but who quite enjoys attending a sale if it is convenient to do so. The word was also used to mean a strumpet or harlot – but that *was* a long time ago.

**Organiser**
Someone with whom the buck stops; the person in overall charge of all aspects of a jumble sale.

**Controller**
The person bullied by the organiser into running one stall or attraction at a jumble sale. Normally found hunting in packs.

**Helper**
Very often a jumble-bug who has wheedled his or her

11

way into the privileged position of being among the first to root through the booty as it arrives at the hall. This person has no authority – just a willingness to help. Often seen helping behind this stall . . . then that one . . . and the one over there. The helper may not have any affinity with the cause for which the sale is being held.

## White Elephant

Originally one of the sacred elephants of Siam, who did no work and was therefore completely useless; its name has long described any unwanted object and is perversely significant as the part of the jumble sale most people fight to get to first.

## Stall

Each category of jumble for sale is awarded the term 'stall' – in this case, unlike the dictionary definition, it has little to do with the table on which goods are displayed and you may often find a rail of clothes called the Nearly New stall, while on the floor may be ranged the Shoes and Handbags stall.

## Trestle

Originally referring to a board placed on two sets of crossed wooden legs, the term has moved on to include folding tables of all kinds, and now any table bearing jumble.

## Prestige stalls

Those stalls displaying superior goods donated to the jumble sale: new, nearly new, classic and antique items, food and garden produce, games and lotteries.

## The Great Rush

The much anticipated, much feared (depending on where you're standing) dash for the first bargains that takes place the second the doors open.

## Dealers

As used in the sentence 'The ruddy dealers got there first' and usually spoken with venom. Dealers – professional buyers of second-hand goods – are proficient at talking prospective but doubtful customers into buying what they have for sale, and innocent jumble sale organisers into letting them have a preview of the event; hence the condemnation.

## Booters

These are the people most likely to use disparaging terms about dealers (hissed through clenched teeth) but are none the less amateur dealers themselves, though it takes a brave soul to say it to their faces. This is because most of them are simply jumble-bugs at heart whose homes become too small to contain the results of years of jumbling. Faced with the trilemma of moving to a bigger house, getting rid of some of the bargains or, dare it be said, giving up jumbling for ever, they choose the easier, middle option and begin selling the excess stuff at car boot sales. This, they find, gives them far more liberty at jumble sales, where they are able to buy anything and everything that takes their fancy without thought for size, style or colour because they can always sell it again, and for a good profit. Booting has become a way of life for many jumblers, but never call them dealers – dear me, no!

**PART ONE: BEHIND THE TRESTLE**

# CHAPTER ONE

## Why Hold a Jumble Sale?

Quite simply because it is the easiest and cheapest way of fundraising. It may be argued that knocking on doors and asking for money is even easier, but for this you need a licence, police certificate or exemption from the Home Office. You also need people motivated enough by the cause to spend a lot of time and energy begging and, whereas the Red Cross or Cancer Relief are charities likely to meet with general approval on the doorstep, a request for 'something towards the boys' club's new football kit' may be greeted with a demoralising ungenerosity – at every asking if you interrupt television or the evening meal. And if you have been sent to collect in the street where those very boys have been riding their motorcycles late at night you will be lucky to get out unscathed.

The jumble sale, however, can be collecting for The Outer Mongolian Yak Dealers' Deodorant Fund and still the customers will come – for a jumble addict or 'jumble-bug' the cause only indicates possible quantity and quality of merchandise. Happily, the person asking for jumble at the doorstep can consider himself or herself to be performing a public service, thus lessening the 'cringe factor' behind the asking, and can even be proud of being part of this country's recycling policy. Perhaps the day will come when the truly green consumer will admit to wearing nothing but second-hand clothes.

No other fundraiser is as flexible as a jumble sale – fêtes and bazaars fail if they don't contain all the aspects tradition dictates, but a jumble can be simply one table in someone's home, designed to raise a few pounds from friends and neighbours for the organiser's favourite charity, and be a great success. A sale of old toys in a front garden can keep a whole estateful of children occupied for an afternoon towards the end of the summer holidays, whilst providing lessons on selling, sharing and charity. A sale can be 'Grand', 'Super' or 'Bumper', it can have a Cake stall, Raffle, Toiletries and Nearly New – or none of these; it can sell refreshments varying from tins of cola and packets of crisps or simple tea and biscuits, to sandwiches, pies, pastries and cakes. It can even be country-wide, like BBC television's Blue Peter and women's magazine sales, and involve thousands of volunteers spending a great many hours sorting tons of stock sent in by viewers and readers.

Some people love to be involved, enjoying the camaraderie of the sort-out, giggling over huge bloomers or a whispy G-string, feeling absurdly important and self-conscious standing behind their stall or sharing the righteousness of the final clearing-up, while for others giving two large bagfuls of what they didn't particularly need can induce a suitably charitable glow without the sharp chill of sacrifice (very cosy). Yet others can give something they know has an intrinsic value – but not too much as it will be wasted with the prices jumblers are prepared to pay. This latter group needs to feel piously self-sacrificial and can fool themselves into believing it a great wrench to give away Grannie's Spode plate with the almost invisible hairline crack, the fact that it doesn't match their highly modern decor being incidental.

The reason there are not more jumble sales lies with uncomprehending worthies, unmoved by the lure of the trestle, who shake their heads and proclaim 'boring' when one is suggested. 'Didn't we have one last year?' they demand, 'Shouldn't we come up with something new?' and spend whole meetings considering sponsored downhill trout-fishing or a sushi-and-sake evening, not realising for one moment how others' passionate need of the jumble sale rests with them. Such people have something lacking in either make-up or education and should be taken gently by the hand, led to some quiet spot and told how one third of the population is relying on them to feed their jumbling addiction; better still, they should be given a book called *The Jumble Sale Handbook* and told to read the chapter entitled on 'Why Hold a Jumble Sale?' I hear it's quite informative.

# CHAPTER TWO

## Insurance – or Dire Warnings No.1 (Not to be Glossed Over)

Oh, alas and alack, I must now qualify all my enthusiastic recommendations by pointing out that there are people who really should think twice about this method of fundraising. In these highly litigious days consideration must be given to accident and its consequences, for a good-hearted gesture may turn into the worst nightmare should somebody damage himself or herself whilst shopping or helping at your jumble sale.

Let me begin on the positive side. You are probably fairly safe if you are raising funds for a registered charity, but even then you should *never* assume that you can just go ahead and hold your sale without consultation or reassurance. Most major charities such as Oxfam and Cancer Relief carry comprehensive Public Liability insurance, and members of societies like the Women's Institute pay for insurance in their subscriptions; but to hold a sale without informing the beneficiaries that you are about to do so and checking with them that you are solidly covered for all events, is naïve, careless or both.

It may be lovely to imagine yourself, the hero, marching through the foyer of the offices of your favourite charity, various acolytes and newspaper photographers at your heels, and asking at the desk in confident voice for the Managing Director – who will trip downstairs with great enthusiasm at the surprise you have sprung, to accept your yard-long cardboard cheque with admiration and gratitude. But you could instead be sidling in through the side door, alone, bowed, enquiring for the MD in a voice husky with trepidation – with a paltry bag of coins in your pocket and a very sad old 'good news – bad news' joke running and re-running through your brain: 'Here's the good news, we had a jumble sale and made £3.42 for your charity. The bad news is that that was all we could save from the fire after the clothes spontaneously combusted. . . .' And to take the matter further, imagine receiving an official letter that states:

> In consultation with our insurers it has been brought to our notice that clause seven of our policy referring to Public Liability requires that we have four full weeks prior notice of any fundraising event. . . .

or:

> We regret that our insurance covers events organised by authorised officers of the society only. . . .

Check, check and triple check; you may be thought odd but you won't be wrong, or bankrupt. For when checking you may well find that those people who should know, don't – and show a remarkable lack of efficiency in finding out. The following tale is completely true, only the names have been changed to protect the guilty.

The village fête had, for many years, been held in a large garden, run in accordance with a vague tradition reinforced by constant use; and the organisational meetings followed exactly the same format each year. However, the time came when the erstwhile hosts decided 'enough is enough' and another garden venue was sought, found, discussed and agreed upon – the new host stating at the first meeting, reasonably enough, that he would rather like to know what insurance cover existed for the event. Representatives of the church and the village hall (who would share the proceeds) were most reassuring as they were both certain that their policies covered anything that could possibly go wrong – double indemnity, in fact.

However, the new host had not risen to the position of owning a garden large enough to accommodate stalls, marquee, brass band and most of the neighbourhood by leaving important questions vaguely answered, so from time to time over the next few months he asked for a simple, headed piece of paper saying that, should anything untoward happen during the setting-up, running and dismantling of the fête, he and his family would not be held responsible or expected to meet any costs or damages. He asked Fred, who told him to phone Penny, who said she thought Bill held the policy, who said that, as far as he knew the secretary, Lucy, had it, who said she believed Cyril knew where it was, who said he really ought to speak to Fred . . . and Lucy said to Bill wasn't it a lot of fuss about nothing, and Bill tutted to Jack and Rhona (who

had hosted the fête for the past nineteen years) that *they* had never made such a silly to-do; but some people had read the report in the newspaper of the woman who had successfully sued for £10,000 damages for breaking her ankle at a garden fête eight years before. And the prospective host grew very short-tempered indeed. Three weeks before the big day he stamped his foot and said 'No cover – no fête'. So Fred phoned Cyril, who sighed and phoned the church's insurance company whose representative smarmed: 'Why, the Parochial Council is *perfectly* covered, Mr er . . . um, have no worries on that score – full Public Liability cover for the tent and stalls. And er, of course, if anyone trips over a paving stone or something, well, between you and me, we can generally lump all responsibility for that onto the bloke who owns the garden. . . .'

Now, I know that a jumble sale is not as ambitious as a full-blown garden fête and possibly not so set about with hazards, but there are risks attendant on any event involving the public that should be appreciated by the organisers, and any group or society about to benefit from a jumble sale should be able to produce their insurance policy on request, preferably by a member who can explain it.

But what if they can't (or can't be bothered) or you know your good cause carries no insurance? Perhaps you are collecting to send a poor, sick child to America for an operation, or your heart has been touched by the plight of refugees, or flood victims, or you just think it would be nice to take local pensioners on a coach trip. This is where

choice of venue for your sale can be very important. A lot of halls carry only the most basic insurance; in simple terms, if Mrs Bloggs trips over the wobbly doorstep her claim for damages is covered, but if a helper negligently drops a cabbage leaf and Mrs Bloggs slips on that you may be in trouble. If the leg of the trestle table snaps off and showers people with broken glass you can probably rest easy, but if it can be proved that the collapse was due to careless erection of the table, start worrying. And if Mrs Nib's cakes strike down half the village with food poisoning you can hardly blame the hall's insurers if they shrug their shoulders and say 'nothing to do with us'.

On the other hand, some halls carry splendidly comprehensive cover, for which you may be asked to contribute a nominal fee of fifty pence or even a pound or two; and if management have made this positive move their agent (or caretaker) will probably be quick to tell you so and back his or her words with hard facts. Let's hope the insurers have produced a paper that everyone can read and understand.

Even professional insurance services recommend that you search for a hall with this sort of cover rather than pay for a comparatively expensive policy for your event – possibly more than £35 which, with the cost of the hall, may be more than the profit you make. *You* may be convinced that your sale has all the ingredients of a block-busting money spinner and can afford the cost of a separate policy, but so were the people who had arranged a weekday afternoon jumble sale in an area ripe with bored young mums just dying for some entertainment; unfortunately the afternoon they chose was also that of an exciting Wimbledon tennis match and the mums all elected to be entertained by their television sets!

The importance of adequate insurance when dealing with the public may be brought home by the information that basic Public Liability, which has generally been fixed at £1,000,000, is now believed to be far too low. And that does not include theft cover, which only applies to locked buildings and places where the general public are not allowed.

Having found your seemingly perfect hall you should check the terms of hiring, for while you may be safe enough from the wrath of your public, a third party liability insurance may mean that your helpers' and your own property, the fixtures and fittings of the hall and the building itself are not insured against damage during your hiring period. You can't do a lot to alter that but, once warned, you can take more care.

# CHAPTER THREE

## *The First Committee Meeting*

Having made the decision to hold a jumble sale, the atmosphere of your meeting will lighten immeasurably and some people may even begin those shuffling movements prior to pushing off home. *Now* is the moment to insist on appointing an organiser, and if you want the job – say so. Even if you don't want it but, on the default of everyone else, accept it anyway, make absolutely clear to the committee that you will take full responsibility only if you have full authority and that you must assume both immediately. Otherwise, as the meeting runs down like an old clock, debate might go something like this:

'Right, so a jumble sale it is. I suppose the Methodist Hall will do. Fred, you live just up the road from it – you'll pop in and make arrangements, won't you?' asks the chairman, with only faint concern.

'I'm on nights all next week, then I've got a few days holiday – but I'll try and see the caretaker in a couple of weeks. When do you want me to book for?' Fred gazes questioningly around the circle of faces.

The chairman is definite. 'Make it a Saturday in about six weeks' time, that will bring it into August.'

'Well, I can't make mornings,' one gruff voice intones, and a higher, more refined one counters, 'But you know afternoons are impossible for me.' The two protagonists glare at one another.

'I'll be in the south of France in six weeks' time,' smugly boasts a third member. 'And my husband and I will be in Skegness,' adds another, nodding and clearly pleased to be siding with the previous speaker. Fred, who has had time to consider, adds, 'I think we're going to a wedding on the wife's side o' the family that weekend.'

By now the chairman is getting cross. He doesn't care when they hold their blasted jumble sale, anyway – he won't be going, can't stand the things. 'Arrange it for next week, then, or two months' time – or two years. I don't know,' he explodes, throwing up his hands in exasperation. 'See what the caretaker has to say.' And he shuffles his papers in a manner that says 'I am going home' and brooks no argument. So, although no one is really that interested and it all seems such a long way off ('My dear, I'll help on the day, of course' . . .), the chairman's hopeful 'Er, if there isn't any other business I'll bring this meeting to a close. Next meeting . . .' is greeted with relief. And the pubs are still open! Some of the members may wonder, as they gather coats, bags and umbrellas, how the event will ever be arranged, but mostly they suppose it will come about 'somehow' – almost as if they still believe in fairies.

Fred, exhilarated by his few days in Blackpool, has,

inevitably, forgotten to contact the caretaker of the hall until two days before the next meeting, which he won't be attending because of a pressing darts match. The chairman reads out 'apologies for absence' and for the first time notices the note attached to Fred's:

Spoke to Caretaker of Methodist Hall. Says he's fully booked with weddings on Saturdays until second week in September except for Sat 3rd Aug. in the morning but we'd have to be out by 11.30.

There are two Friday evenings we can have it – Aug 2nd + Aug 9th when the Scouts are at Camp.

Yours
Fred.

'Huh,' he grunts, 'so what do you suggest we do? Mrs Read, you'll be in charge again, I trust? What do *you* say?'

Mrs Read has been waiting for this with some trepidation. 'Actually, this time I rather thought someone else . . . my arthritis, you know . . . and Harold and I are visiting our daughter in Canada in November, I don't think we will have time. . . .'

'Well, I must say, Mrs Read, I do think you could have told us earlier,' pouts the chairman, petulantly; then, to the body of the hall, 'Who would like to take over?' Silence. 'Oh, come on!'

A tentative voice says, 'If only we knew when it was to be, see. I've got this part-time job until the end of the summer, otherwise. . . .'

'I wouldn't mind after the kids go back to school,' offers someone else, while a brisk, well-known organiser type vetoes the only Saturday the Methodist Hall is free with a firm 'August the third is impossible, it's the day of the Church Fête, no one will go to a jumble sale.' This from Miss Wilkes, organiser of the Church Fête, of course. 'Friday the ninth, in the evening, I could manage.'

'Fridays are no good for me,' cuts in the man with the gruff voice, envisaging the ragging he would get from his drinking partners if he had to miss a session for so silly a reason. The chairman tries to call the meeting to order. 'OK, OK,' he mouths placatingly, 'we'll leave the sale until September though, I must say, it's a poor do. Still if none of you can find time. . . .' He looks down at his papers as his heavy sarcasm finds its mark.

In the ensuing silence a small voice drops, 'Perhaps we

could hold it somewhere else?' The suggestion is mulled over, and a few alternatives suggested – gruff voice opting for the pub skittle alley. Three or four volunteers offer to find out when such places will be available and it is agreed, with relief on the part of most, to shelve the decision on the organiser until all the reports are in. This would normally be in a month's time but, as August holidays mean it would be difficult to scare up even a quorum of members, the problem must rest – as heavy as stodgy bread pudding on a weak stomach – until the September meeting.

For the squeamish among you let me say immediately I have no intention of illustrating the September meeting, for even the least imaginative must realise what a Medusa's head of snakes it must turn out to be. If that group couldn't co-ordinate one person with one venue, how on earth will they manage with half a dozen? Instead I shall take you back to the June meeting and offer a portrayal of how it could turn out, whilst trying to avoid idealising the situation. Here goes:

'Right, so a jumble sale it is. Now, Mrs Read, dare, dare we call upon you again as organiser?'

'I'm very sorry, Mr Chairman, but I really can't do it this time. My arthritis and. . . .'

The chairman cuts through her obvious embarrassment. 'Oh, Mrs Read, what a pity! We *shall* miss you. You've done a splendid job in the past.' He makes a note on his pad about a little something to show the club's appreciation for all the hard work, etc. Looking up, he beams at his audience. 'May I have some suggestions for a successor for Mrs Read, someone with efficiency, intelligence, imagination . . . Mr Brown?'

'Well, no, not me,' grins Brown, ruefully, as the others chuckle, 'but I'd like to suggest Miss Walsh.' Miss Walsh pulls a face at him and says she's sure there's someone far better than her. There is a silence and in a rare moment of telepathy all minds but one conjure up the vision of bossy, overwhelming, frightening Miss Wilkes and are linked in a communal, imaginary groan. Inevitably, the dreaded one speaks.

'Well, there's nothing for it, I'll just have to do it myself. As you all know, I've had considerable experience of organising,' says Miss Wilkes, with an air of finality. She is not a woman over-used to being baulked, contradicted or turned down. The other members to a man recall the jumbles before nice Mrs Read took over and panic spreads among them, but their cunning yet upstanding chairman (a nifty chess player) has seen this coming and is prepared. In syrupy tones he addresses the one who already thinks herself queen of the jumble.

'Miss Wilkes, how very good of you,' he oozes, 'but we couldn't possibly impose, as we know how much time and energy you are spending on the Church Fête, and the Harvest Supper.' She opens her mouth to rebut this and he, very wisely, busies himself in an exaggerated fashion, searching for a face in the sparse crowd of ten. 'Actually, I rather thought . . . Gillian?'

Murmurs of appreciation rise from the committee all round, except from Miss Wilkes who goggles like a fish. Gillian, a cheerful, likeable lady who has an easy but capable manner, is pleased at the almost unanimous verdict and is quite happy to take on the job. She knows she has only to ask the others and they will give her all the help in the world, because they know she will run the event sensibly, without upsetting anyone. The chairman now wisely hands over the whole matter, and a good chunk of the meeting, to her. She opens her notebook and creases the page.

'Right. Now, when and where. I suppose we'd better make it some time in September, what with summer holidays and the Church Fête.' (She inclines her head towards the disappointed Miss Wilkes.) 'I'll check the community diary in the Post Office. Fred, will you ask the Methodist Hall caretaker what Saturdays he has free, and what he's charging? Enid, if you can do the same at the Community Centre – and if someone can ask about the skittle alley?' Gradually she works her way through all the possible venues. 'And I would like all answers by the end of next week, so I can make a decision and a firm booking by the next meeting.'

'You know I can't do mornings,' owns gruff voice.

'That's all right, Basil, if I do choose a morning I'm sure you will be invaluable in other ways. Maybe you could help collecting jumble,' she says in a firm but friendly voice. No one else tries to influence her decision with their domestic arrangements, and Fred makes a mental note to corner the caretaker in the pub that very evening.

# CHAPTER FOUR

## *When? And Where?*

You probably think your group is operating free will when you choose the date for your jumble sale. You are mistaken. The fundraising calendar is as rigid as the church calendar, and is often dependent upon it. The first jumbles always begin mid-January; for who wants to organise anything earlier, immediately after all the work involved over Christmas and the New Year? February and March are high season, absolute bliss for jumble-bugs, but the peak is dependent upon Easter, be it early or late, for then begin the Easter fayres and bazaars. The number of jumble sales lessens as summer fêtes and fairs, fun days and steam rallies multiply – and these are of a totally different category. Everyone you count on as staff is away, not cleverly all at the same time but at staggered intervals, and are so involved with the larger local events that any idea of a jumble will get scant attention. Until mid-September, that is; and with the children back at school there comes the mini-season, lasting until the start of the Christmas bazaars in November. The bazaars sell painted

*'I know it's the quiet period, but . . .'*

23

stones and knitted tea-cosies to be given as gifts and as such are superior to the humble jumble, but there will still be a smattering of the latter until a fortnight before Christmas, when everything goes quiet and the fundraising world draws breath.

## Co-ordinating Time and Place

At first, 'where' and 'when' will appear obvious: 'Well, it's got to be the Church Hall on Saturday, such-and-such a date, hasn't it?' And so thought a dozen other groups, as you will discover when reading your local paper's 'What's On' section for that week.

Given someone to organise it, there are three essentials for every jumble sale: a place to hold it, a quantity of stock and a crowd of customers, (even helpers are not vital; one person can run a jumble sale by sitting at the door taking entrance money and charging for each bag carried out) and of the three the most important is customers. You can lay out the contents of a stately home on your trestles but you will not make money without people to buy them, and people will only come to your sale if it is at the right place at the right time. Different locations warrant different approaches.

## Town Jumbles

The ideal urban situation is in a high or main street on a Saturday morning, Saturday afternoon – or all day if you can raise the stock and have the stamina. Is there an empty shop you can hire? Or a church hall fronting the main street with room to have a few stalls outside to draw custom? Second best at the height of either of the two seasons is a venue within walking distance of the main shopping area and close to other likely jumble sales; the true jumble-bug will be bound to fit you into the itinerary, especially if you have been clever about time.

Good timing, arranged some weeks in advance, depends on information and insight: information being how other organisers are planning their sales, whether there seems to be a pattern to the grouping of the halls used, and if one hall is used more often than the others – why?; insight being a knowledge of the minds of those you wish to attract to your event.

If, at the height of the season, you peruse your local paper, you will find you are invited to attend sales in many parts of town, not to mention those in the suburbs and outlying villages. The times stated will be on the hour or the half-hour during the day, beginning at 9.30 and leaving a gap for lunch; and the greatest number of sales will open at 10.30 or 11.00, with a considerable number starting at 2.00 or 2.30 in the afternoon, by which time, the organiser hopes, morning jumblers will have regained stamina from a good meal and their purses an injection of cash.

Now consider the mind of the practised jumble-bug, for whom the first ten minutes of a jumble sale are paramount. He or she will also have closely studied the local newspaper, and, armed with a map of the town, a note of other sales advertised on posters, and a knowledge of areas and charities likely to provide the best – or the fewest – bargains, will plot a route with a cunning and expertise worthy of an SAS operation. Whereas any normal mortal wishing to go from hall A to hall B in the shortest possible time would leap into the car, join the rest of the Saturday traffic in the tedium of traffic lights, zebra crossings and one-way-only routes which add a mile to the journey, then take more valuable time circling a car park in a seemingly eternal search for a soon-to-be-vacated place, the true devotee will stow the bargains from the first jumble sale in the car (parked, with forethought, in exactly the right place) and set off, at a brisk walk, for hall B. Neatly swerving around dawdling window shoppers, passing unhesitatingly through shops with convenient rear exits, diving down alleyways unknown to most and following unpeopled back streets (but never breaking into a trot), our jumble-bug will arrive, only slightly out of breath, in about the time it takes anyone else to purchase and affix a 'Pay and Display' car park ticket.

However, this tactician of the trestles will also know when it is worthwhile to use the car to nip over to a juicy little better-class sale on the other side of town, of course with great stress on arriving there for that vital first ten minutes. Occasionally the temptation to put a nose round the door of a sale long in progress, just to see what's left, proves irresistible, but only if it sits on a direct line between the previous one and the next one or when all others have been exhausted.

But what, you may ask, of other sorts of customers? Yes, you will have people who live in the area, those without transport, friends of the cause and some just with time to kill, but if their hearts don't quicken at the thought of all that jumble to sort through then they will only see before them a pile of junk, and nobody wastes time sorting through junk, or spends hard-earned money buying it, do they? Few of these customers will want to be bothered with an early morning jumble sale, and whether they turn up at all can be dependent on the rest of the family's programme for the day, how soon they can get through Sainsbury's, what's on TV, and the weather.

In other words, in the heart of town rely on the jumble-bug, and if you are looking for a quick turnover on jumble only, organise a 9.00 or 9.30 sale, with stock arranged in as easily accessible a way as possible. Your customer will have queued, possibly for forty-five minutes, and *needs* to buy something to justify such an expenditure of time before rushing on to the next sale. And don't complicate the early morning jumble sale with Teas or a Raffle (unless you are very clever and sell them to your customers as they wait in the queue beforehand). The tea will keep a few locals around but they won't spend much more at your trestles, and the Raffle will be a disappointment with just the helpers and tea drinkers waiting for the numbers to be drawn. Likewise, a Cake stall will fail at an early sale as the jumble-bug is not likely to want the bother of carrying a fragile, cream-filled, three-egg sponge in the hurly-burly of the headlong dash at the next three venues. However, tea and cakes go down very well at a later event when, exhausted and probably triumphant, the jumbler has fulfilled his or her Saturday morning's brief – usually towards the end of an 11.00 or 11.30 sale, or in the afternoon. Then, if a Raffle catches the eye whilst the tea is still hot . . . it *is* very difficult to wind down and stop spending . . . and as it won't be long before the draw takes place . . . well, might as well have another rummage. . . . (On the subject of refreshments, see Chapter Seven, 'Is it Legal?', section on the production of food for sale.)

From the organiser's point of view, the running of the early Saturday sale is most suited to groups of young and vigorous people for whom it is just one event in a busy day and who appreciate a quick 'layout' followed by as brief a selling time as possible. The later, more leisurely sale is preferred by older groups, predominantly female, who like to lavish time and thought on preparation, look forward to it as a social event and enjoy practising their sales technique. Indeed, a lot of helpers of all ages find they can be far more extrovert than their characters would normally allow, when they stand behind a trestle for a cause.

So, given that you have decided what sort of sale suits your group, and made a careful choice of mid-town hall, now you need to make the customers spend their money on *your* collection of jumble rather than that of someone else down the road. A sneaky trick that may work in your favour is to time your opening for 9.45, or 10.15 – which will take your advert out of the ordinary and cause no end of a headache for the person who just cannot bear to miss a sale if it is humanly possible to fit it in. If there are three at 11.00, only one can be attended, with no time to mourn the other two, but confuse the issue with one at 10.45 and you can be sure that, should there be the tiniest chance of it being fitted into the schedule, it will be! Or you can cater for the lunchtime crowd, bridging the gap between morning and afternoon sales by starting at 12.30 or 1.00. This is especially easy to arrange if you are fundraising for a club on club premises with a licensed bar adjacent; you don't necessarily have more customers but you have a lot of happy helpers!

It is not advisable to start a Saturday sale any later than 3.00 in the afternoon, for it risks clashing with both helpers' and customers' preparations for an evening's leisure, but an evening sale in town during the week can be a great money-maker as long as the nature of the customer is understood. As there will be no competition to dilute the mixture, a long queue of jumble-bugs (many of them jumble-starved Saturday workers) and dealers in bric-à-brac, with a few bewildered innocents, will begin forming long before your 6.00 or 6.30 start, and the air will bristle with competitive hostility as they flood in through the doors. Raffles and refreshments will be totally ignored as the hordes trample their way unerringly to the White Elephant, Book and Toy stalls, grabbing anything and everything as they go, chanting the familiar cry 'How much?' Woe betide the helper of a nervous disposition who vacillates and stammers instead of snapping back a determined 'Fifty pence'. Organisers would be wise to recruit only the toughest helpers for this sale, offering as consolation the fact that it will all be over very quickly – even dealers won't want to miss their favourite TV 'soap'.

If you are brave enough to opt for such thrills and spills, you would be wise to work doubly hard at collecting the sort of stock the crowd of customers will be lusting after. Faced with a sea of polyester skirts, shrunken woollens and old corsets, relieved only by three Mills & Boon paperbacks, a macramé wall-hanging, seven cracked plates and a rusty cake tin, customers can 'turn nasty' and your toughest helpers become 'bouncers' for the evening.

## Country Jumbles

On the whole these are much more relaxed affairs, relying heavily on local loyalty, plus advertising in shops, pubs, etc., to pull in the customers. The mobile jumble-bug living in the area might well weigh the village sale on its own against half a dozen in town, taking into account petrol and parking, possible quality of purchases, mood and weather. Maybe he or she will spend a hectic morning doing the town jumbles and then enjoy a relaxing afternoon just down the road in the village after a snack lunch at home. What may scupper a country jumble is a clashing event within a three-mile radius – a car boot sale, garden fête or bazaar; it is worth finding out if your post office or community school keeps a diary which you can check for free dates, then enter that of your sale. If neither does, why not suggest it and benefit everyone?

The more remote and tucked away your venue, the less patronage you will receive (unless you already have a reputation in the area for good-quality clothes or extra-delicious cakes), so ask the hall caretaker when booking how well jumble sales normally go in that locality and be prepared to consider somewhere else. Perhaps the next village is two shops larger and busier with a hall on the main road? Of course, if your fundraising is for a purely local charity it will have to stay in the village, with less emphasis put on jumble and more on Produce, Raffle, Cakes and other stalls, the more ingenious the better. Then advertise locally like mad. Picket the pub, pin posters on every pole and gate, load the vicar with leaflets and flattery. Tell everyone of the added attractions, so that at least if the purses are few they will be deep.

I know of a village that has one jumble sale a year, no more, but it is prestigious enough to draw the most ardent jumblers, whatever attractions the town puts up to rival it. I also know another, quite large village where local customers (from the avid to the mildly interested) all boycott one yearly sale because the organiser's attitude is so unpleasant. On such things can a country jumble win or lose.

## Suburban Jumbles

Only you can decide whether you have a village community spirit and can command enough local support, whether you are close enough to town to be included in the jumblophile's calculations or whether you need to take a hall in town for maximum custom – bearing in mind it may seem a little odd if a sale in support of St Peter's is held in St James's hall, three miles away.

## Booking the Location

If you are confident of your cause's Public Liability insurance, and are not tied to any one place, don't feel you are restricted to church halls – shop around for the best rates of hire. Try schools, sports clubs, hospital social clubs, pub skittle alleys, empty shops, anywhere that may be rented. I once helped at a sale laid out in a church and had to pew-hop in a most irreverent manner to take the money; but it was fun and I doubt if the church had heard so many ribald comments and so much laughter ever before in its long history.

Be sure to inspect the premises with the caretaker before making a firm booking; it is not unheard of for an unscrupulous type to present a bill for damage not caused during your sale. I don't suggest you study every inch of the place as if about to buy rather than hire, but just enough to show you are a person of forethought and discernment and won't fall for any tricks; let the casual phone booker or the chap who does a deal over a pint in the local pay for the broken socket or cracked loo seat that no one will own to damaging.

Check on what you are getting for your money. Don't just assume you have use of a kitchen, cups, saucers and tea-urn. How many tables are there and are they so old they may collapse under the weight of three pairs of knickers and a donkey jacket? Are there any tables at all? Not such a ridiculous question, as shown by the sad story of one group who hired a lovely bright new hall, by word of mouth only. They arrived just after breakfast time, eager to decant a vast accumulation of black bags from their car boots and carefully iced and wrapped sponge cakes from baskets and boxes. Mrs Smith had ordered extra milk from her milkman for the teas they would be serving and was looking forward to setting down her unwieldy, clanking bagful, while Mrs Jones had made a detour to the shop for another bag of sugar in case one wasn't enough. Mr Philips, the first through the hall door, stood in the centre of the gleaming polished wood floor and sniffed appreciatively at the paint and plaster smells, eyeing the smooth, uncluttered squareness of it all. Nothing marred its new perfection, its magnificent . . . emptiness. He lowered his burden of bin bags to the floor and, briskly rubbing his hands together, suggested to the others who, similarly laden, had crowded in behind him, that they had better set up the trestles. But where were they?

They inspected the hall from top to bottom; they felt along the walls for a secret panel, they trooped in and out of the lavatories, the broom cupboard and the kitchen as if the second or third investigation might reveal a secret hiding place. They even sent out a posse to circle the exterior of the building and check for an outside store. It was as they were beginning to appreciate the horror of the situation – all that jumble and no tables – that the refreshments contingent flung open the kitchen cupboards and discovered a marked lack of china; every shelf was bare.

Frantic action reminiscent of a disturbed ants' nest ensued, with helpers rushing off at full pelt in every direction – some for pasting tables from their loft or garage, others to gather a motley collection of cups, saucers and plates. One enthusiast arrived back at the hall with his kitchen table upside down on his car roof-rack; but nothing could make up for the missing, evenly matched trestles. The final compromise of three sagging pasting tables, two card tables, one folding picnic table and one red formica-topped kitchen table was no match for the acres of jumble that kept on arriving and was soon spread upon that pristine floor. And the tea ladies, when they had time to stop and think, realised that their customers would have to stand up to take their refreshment, for the hall was as little equipped with chairs as it was with tables.

The sale was not a success. The waiting crowd, who had been amused by the frantic activity before the event, soon found their interest in jumble waning when they had to go down on their knees to sort through the clothing, and large piles of the stuff were left unturned to be bundled up and thrown away. What's more, in their disappointment they were not prepared to drink tea standing up and soon drifted off to other sales or their own kitchens. Twenty minutes after the beginning the glum helpers found themselves alone, stranded in a sea of unsold garments, white elephants and fairy cakes.

There are a lot of questions you can put to the caretaker that usually only occur with hindsight, such as 'Why didn't I ask him where the fuse box is?' when you are groping in the dark because an enthusiastic helper has plugged in an old electric fire to see if it works. Because of this I include a check-list, and suggest you take along with you a note of useful questions when you meet the caretaker. For instance, a hall with more than one room, or a school or sports club, may have other groups (such as yoga or flower-arranging classes) booked for the same time, all feeling they have as much right to the kitchen as you. Perhaps the amateur dramatics group are putting on a show that evening and have left the stage set in readiness; imagine the bitter recriminations if all your customers' children decide to play up there, or worse – you manage to sell the props!

Whichever questions you choose to omit, don't leave out 'Are there any hidden clauses or requirements?' Forget this and you wouldn't be the first group to reach the end of the sale and breathe a sigh of sheer exhaustion only to be 'floored' by the caretaker's bombshell. You have struggled to stack the trestles, you have swept the floor and cleared the kitchen, there isn't a scrap of rubbish to be seen and you feel smugly justified in going home to put your feet up – but there at the door he looms, with a wide-eyed look of amazement and a reasonable, but hurt, tone of voice as he enquires why you haven't polished the floor for that night's dance, as he had stipulated when you booked. . . .

Obviously, you are not about to dismiss the hall out of hand just because one or two of your questions receive a negative answer, but you should be able to make a fair comparison of all the likely places and, having made your choice and booked the best, you will know whether to bring chalk or paper and drawing pins for the advertising board (or, indeed, if you need to supply your own board), paper and old towels for the lavatories and extra dustpans and brushes. The latter you will find worth bringing anyway, to make sure the clearing-up is spread fairly amongst staff who, otherwise, will be quick to eye the one single broom in your weary grasp and say, 'Well, you don't need me – I'll be off.'

## Booking the Room – Check-list

### 1 *The 'Contract'*
* Is the cost of hire competitive/satisfactory?
* Is the cost all-inclusive, or do you have to pay more for lighting, heating, use of the urn or china?
* Does the hall carry the sort of insurance your group needs and do you have to pay extra for it?
* Can you see proof of this insurance?
* Are there any hidden clauses or requirements?

### 2 *The Building*
* How much of the building can you use? Kitchen? Lavatories?
* How do you turn on the central heating and the water heater?
* Where are the fuse boxes and stop-cock?
* Is there somewhere safe to put helpers' coats and handbags?

### 3 *The Contents*
* Do you have use of the tea-urn? How does it work?
* What do you do if anything belonging to the hall is broken during your occupation?
* Do the tables and chairs look sturdy and are there enough of them?
* Will they be available on the day?
* Are the lavatories clean and always equipped with paper, soap and towels?
* Can you use brooms and brushes from the caretaker's cupboard?
* Is there a free-standing advertising board to set out on the pavement on the day?
* Is it a blackboard or can posters be pinned onto it?
* Can you put up a poster advertising your sale on a notice-board inside the hall?

### 4 *Time*
* Is the hall available at a time that suits your group – not forgetting laying-out and clearing-up time?
* Can you lay out your sale the night before?
* Will the caretaker be available on the day in case of emergency?

# CHAPTER FIVE

## *The Second Committee Meeting*

When you consider that the average jumble sale, from conception to final rubbish disposal, occupies something like seventy-five man-hours, you realise that, as an organiser, you must be strong enough to make sure the bulk of those hours of work are not performed by you. This committee meeting is your best chance to delegate, and you must arrive for it armed with a firm grasp of all the jobs involved, a flexible idea of who you wish to perform – or 'control' – each one and how they must go about it.

Obviously you will aim to match the person to the job – put someone with a large vehicle in charge of collecting, someone who can draw and spell in charge of posters – but (on behalf of your customers) please consider your helpers' attitudes towards jumble sales and those who attend them, before you allocate control of the various stalls. No amount of reasoning will turn a jumblophobe into a jumblophile, and an atmosphere of contempt or derision from the person doing the selling will soon frighten away custom. Indeed, I know of one group who still have a very grim lady firmly entrenched in the pattern of their yearly sale. She once angrily flew at me as I sifted through the clothing with 'The best things aren't at the bottom of the pile. Take something from the top, pay for it and get out to give someone else a chance.' On another occasion the whole hall had to listen as she kept up a constant diatribe, in booming baritone, against those passing – head down and embarrassed – on the other side of the trestle. She firmly believes that the customers should pay just a little less than the price of the garment when new, and the only reason they are not prepared to is that they are common, vulgar cheats. I once tried to reason with her, pointing out that one didn't know until it was taken home whether an article would fit or if it was worn or damaged. She sniffed and told me I should spend more time inspecting it, ask to try it on in the lavatory – then pay a lot of money for it. . . . Her group's sales now attract so few people that the queue is easily accommodated in the hall's tiny porch before the sale, and when the doors open the stalwart helpers (fewer each year) have a worried, hounded look; but it seems there is no shifting the lady from a role she has made uniquely her own.

If you suspect you may have members with a snobbish or out-of-place attitude to jumblers, there is no reason to turn away their offers of help. Channel their energy into making tea, or running the Raffle – any job where they are not in a position to intimidate the customer. The check-list of jobs to delegate will jog your memory. And you are bound to find some to suit your difficult helper.

Your jumble sale may have no need of some of the

categories on the list and other categories may double up. For instance, the person in charge of collecting stock, having perhaps spent an evening making fairy cakes if there is to be a Cake stall, will probably help with the layout, run a stall and then assist with the final clearing up. On the other hand, no helper should feel isolated in his or her job, so the person in charge of, say, advertising must not feel that either the burden of drawing the posters or that of their distribution falls entirely on him or her.

## Jobs that Require Controllers – Check-list

| | | |
|---|---|---|
| Collecting jumble | Ladies' Clothing | Bran Tub |
| Advertising | Gents' Clothing | Prestige stalls |
| White Elephant | Children's Clothing | Treasurer |
| Toys | Shoes and Handbags | Rubbish disposal |
| Books | Nearly New | Cake stall |
| Household Linen | Raffle | Refreshments |

In an ideal world the second committee meeting would take place three weeks before the sale, which gives just enough time to do everything but not so much that duties may be forgotten. Whenever it takes place it is probably the last time you will have your staff together before the layout – so don't forget, as you thrash out who does what (and find your plans totally disrupted because Mrs Biggs refuses to do Refreshments and Mr Jermyn sulks when you give the White Elephant stall to Mr Ronson), that everyone must know just what is expected of them. There are vital aspects to every duty and every category, and you (probably) or your delegate (if you're lucky) must make sure they are all covered.

## Collecting Jumble

The person in charge of this has a choice of two methods. The first entails the distribution of leaflets which state that members of your group or charity will call on such-and-such a day to collect jumble for a sale to take place on . . . (give date, time and location), and then the organisation of a working party to collect on the day specified from the houses canvassed. By the second method, advertisements asking for jumble are pinned on local notice-boards, with the addresses of people who will be available to take in and store the stock and the telephone number of someone willing to collect from those who can't deliver. Either way, the leaflet or advertisement must carry the name of the group for whom you are raising funds: this is a legal requirement.

Jumble should be stored in a dry, airy place or it will very soon smell musty and be totally unsaleable. For this reason, it is unwise to take on the left-overs of another jumble sale. The more persuasive the donors the more desperate they must be; you can be sure that what they offer has been festering for a month or two in the dampest corner of a garage.

It would also be wise, before embarking on a collecting spree, to find out what can or cannot legally be sold (some basic guidelines are given in Chapter Seven). It is most infuriating for the collector, having accepted some bulky electrical item, stored it in his or her hallway where everyone barked their shins on it, struggled to get it in and out of the car and finally arrived at the White Elephant stall, to be informed that as it has the old red, green and black wires it can't be put up for sale. And the collector is stuck with it. Far better not to accept it in the first place.

## Advertising

See the next chapter, which is devoted to this subject.

## White Elephant and Toys

Those in control of either of these stalls should not, if they wish to make a success of them, leave to chance the quantity and quality of stock that might turn up on the day. They must either work with the collecting party or tout for the goods themselves.

Chapter Seven is relevant to the running of these stalls.

## Books

Unless they are of a pornographic nature, books, on the whole, tend to stay on the right side of the law. The only problem the controller of this stall may have is making them stay on the table. I suggest that a number of sturdy, low-sided cardboard trays, previously used to transport fruit and vegetables, are collected by helpers between now and the sale.

## Household Linen, Clothing and Shoes and Handbags

The controllers of these stalls have no duties to perform until the layout time. Put them to work in other areas.

## Nearly New

The controller of this stall should be prepared to set up a working party during the week before the sale to vet the incoming jumble, pick out the best and launder it, or to wait until the layout and just iron the best as it comes to light. The sad rows of bedraggled garments merely pulled from the heap and thrown onto hangers that one sees at so many jumbles are depressing in the extreme and do nothing to increase sales. This stall really requires forethought and discussion. Does anyone know from where to borrow or rent a dress rail, or is there some convenient feature of the hall that will accept hangers? Does the controller feel confident to set the prices of the garments or should the committee set a guideline – say, £3 for a suit?

Finally, here is a brief reminder of things the person running the Nearly New stall might need to take to the layout: iron and ironing board; white cloth to cover a trestle; tape measure for those clothes that have lost their size label; sticky labels, or paper and pins, and a pen for pricing the garments; plastic bags for attractive presentation of the goods on the table; and bags into which to pack the sold items to maintain the illusion of a superior service.

## Raffle

Another decision for the committee to make: will some money be set aside to buy prizes, or will the collecting party be expected to ask those already donating jumble to 'give something for the Raffle'? Or might your Raffle supremo be happy to ask local businesses to donate a prize? You could, of course, leave it in the lap of the gods and see what arrives on the day; and if the selection proves to be mean you could 'divert' a cake from the Cake stall.

The more pleasantly arranged a Raffle is, the more attention it attracts, so your controller should bring a cloth for the table and be encouraged to think of anything else to make it interesting: perhaps an odd or amusing article from which to draw the winners. At least one book of cloakroom tickets, easily available from stationers and newsagents, is essential, and if more than one book is needed they must be of different colours – nothing will console Mrs Jones if both she and Mrs Brown have a red number ninety-nine, but Mrs Brown takes the prize because the small numbers at the top of her ticket match those on the one drawn.

There are legal requirements for a Raffle, not least one which states that tickets may only be sold at the time and place of the event. Chapter Seven contains advice on this.

## Bran Tub

A pleasant diversion for small children that need not be a tub, nor need it contain anything as messy as bran. At its simplest, a brightly covered cardboard boxful of newspaper confetti is all that is needed as a base and a supply of small, inexpensive toys and sweets roughly wrapped in tissue as prizes. The problem with this attraction is making it pay; even the youngest child is street-wise enough to know what he or she should be getting for ten pence; the solution is to find a Cash and Carry warehouse and appeal to the charity of the manager. There may be boxes of jelly 'creepy-crawlies' and bright pink false teeth at the price your local sweet shop pays; and if they can make a profit so can you. In another part of the warehouse may be large packs of novelties at the right price – party masks and hooters, pretend wristwatches, balloons, as wide a choice as could be wished. The temptation here is to buy too much, and thought must be given to the likely number of small customers; one box each of sweets and a toy equally acceptable to boy or girl, toddler or ten-year-old, generally proves to be enough; but the emphasis must be on safety, for mothers' attention will be firmly fixed in other directions.

## Prestige Stalls

You must decide whether you need to hold attractions other than the ones above, and that decision will be dependent on location, time of year and nature of your group. For instance, a gardening club would be rather foolish not to rely heavily on its plants and cut flowers as a source of profit. One of your number may be enthusiastically in favour of a Toiletries or Handicrafts stall. But beware: if your group holds summer fêtes and Christmas bazaars, one of these could be but a few weeks away and the items sold at jumble sale prices will deplete the stock for the more lucrative events.

The following list contains a few ideas for Prestige stalls.

| | |
|---|---|
| New Toys | Produce (packets, tins, jars) |
| Jewellery | Guess the Weight/Name Games |
| Tombola | Pin-in-a-map Treasure Hunt |
| Toiletries | Plants |
| Handicrafts | |

Whatever stalls you opt for, point out to your controller that superior goods sell best if they are beautifully presented; thought given to setting and arrangement pays off.

## Treasurer

Five minutes before your jumble sale begins is not the time to realise you have no small change, for you can be sure your first customers will all proffer £1 coins for ten-penny purchases. At least £5 in small change from bank or post office will be required, plus a handful of those small plastic money bags to fill with all your lovely profit.

## Rubbish Disposal

When all is over and the unsold jumble has been crammed back into boxes and bags, you and your helpers will probably feel like the Disciples as they cleared up after feeding the five thousand. But at least the twelve biblical baskets of crumbs could be fed to the animals, while the disposal of your more substantial left-overs could prove to be a major problem. To begin with, you most certainly can't pile them up outside the hall, for even if the caretaker doesn't hold strong views on the subject, the fire authorities do. Then, a lot of people are under the impression that charity shops will be grateful for any old junk and will be happy to take charge of several carloads of bags and boxes at the end of a busy Saturday afternoon. Mild-mannered and kindly though the ladies and gents who run these shops may appear, being used as nothing more than a rubbish tip, time after time during the jumble season, has a tendency to sour their dispositions, and the terms they may use when advising you what to do with your left-overs can be a little startling.

And the end of the sale is not the time to begin looking for someone to take the rubbish away. For a start, you may be surprised to find that the old rag-and-bone man doesn't exist any more, and fevered study of the *Yellow Pages* will lead you a rare old dance – from 'Rag Merchants' to 'See also Cleaning Rags and Waste', from there to 'Cleaning Materials Mfrs and Suppliers' and so on – none of them available to answer the telephone at 5 o'clock on a Saturday afternoon. Even if someone thinks ahead and phones during weekday working hours they may meet with little success as, for a long time now, sorting cotton waste from man-made has proved unprofitable for these businesses. But the 'green' movement is attracting more and more of the smart money and recycling is a growth industry; at least one company now produces woven cloth containing eighty per cent recycled wool and you may be lucky enough to have in your area one of the enterprises that are being set up to supply similar mills. A phone call to the Citizens' Advice Bureau could be the solution, for they may have the numbers of such businesses, other environmentally aware groups recycling for charity or individuals who will sell what they can for profit and dispose of the rest.

Alternatively, you will have to arrange for someone to take it all to the municipal rubbish tip or find another jumble sale organiser foolish enough to take it on.

## Selling Food

Already set about by rules and shortly to be even more tightly strait-jacketed, this subject will require investigation before you know whether or not you can legally sell cakes, conserves or refreshments to the public. The greater part of Chapter Seven is concerned with this aspect and should be studied closely; you may find your group has been registered as a business and as such is bound by the same laws that control the biggest food producers in the Common Market. However, if, having read the advice, you then believe you can safely go ahead and appoint controllers, there are some very important points to be made when telling them how their jobs must be handled:

### Cake Stall

The controller of the Cake stall first has to commission the making of cakes, pies, tarts and quiches for the stall and is obliged by law to ensure they come from clean kitchens – difficult though it may be to turn down an offer from ladies such as nice Mrs Bull just because she lets the cats sit on the work surface watching her cook. Perishable ingredients must be kept by the cooks in their refrigerators with the resulting goodies transported well covered and away from jumble; *and they must remain covered right through the sale*. When sold they must be put into new paper or plastic bags.

The person in charge of this stall needs a lot of experience and common sense. There is a limit to the number of rich fruit cakes which will go as 'impulse buys' in a small community, so the sort of stock that will turn up on the day must not be left to chance. A nice mix should be specified of iced sponges, small buns, fruit cakes, fruit or jam tarts and tartlets, large and small savoury flans and quiches, shortbread or other biscuits and home-made sweets. Very often the cooks are happier knowing exactly what is wanted of them than just being told to 'bring a cake'.

The goodies should be brought to the hall immediately prior to the sale, to keep them as fresh as possible, and the stall controller (neatly aproned) should have a trestle spread with a sparkling white cloth ready to receive them. Nothing should be displayed uncovered nor, since medical opinion has come out so firmly against it, closely wrapped in clingfilm; however, clingfilm remains a useful transparent covering and can safely be used so long as it does not come into contact with foods with a fat content –

which most of the items on this stall will have. For instance, a gloriously squidgy iced cake can be shown off to perfection in a clean biscuit tin, with clingfilm stretched across the top, clear of the surface of the cake; and later, with the tin lid clamped in place, the whole will make a convenient parcel for the customer to carry home – charge a little extra for the privilege! Members of your group, if asked in good time, are sure to come up with unwanted biscuit tins, often kept as too good and useful to throw away. The local baker may be pleased to donate some cardboard cake boxes that can be covered with clingfilm in the same manner, or you could consider constructing your own see-through lids in the best Blue Peter tradition. Cut strips of card from cereal boxes, curve into rings, secure with staples or sellotape and cover with yet more clingfilm. The cake can be put on a paper plate then topped with one of these lids with no harm to the decoration underneath, and no health hazard to those who eat it. Ordinary plastic bags, at the time of writing, have no such tainted reputation and can happily be wrapped around solid fruit cakes and, failing any of the above suggestions, ballooned around fragile, gooey concoctions. Small cakes and sweets can also be bagged in polythene, in varying amounts, and ready priced.

Complying with the rules and making sure that the Cake stall looks, and is, as clean as possible not only avoids possible trouble with Authority but will be appreciated by customers who are more likely to sample your wares if they see them protected from the dust all around.

## Refreshments

Very similar rules apply here to those for the Cake stall and, indeed, you may even decide that local cooks would be better employed making small cakes and gâteaux to be cut into portions and sold with tea and coffee, than having their wares sold on a separate stall (you can always have some paper bags standing by for those who want to take their treat home). Or perhaps a large feature of your Saturday lunchtime jumble sale will be home-made soup and sandwiches, prepared by volunteers either in their own kitchens or in the one at the hall. Even if you find yourself restricted because of lack of hot water or other regulations, a box of packets of crisps and a case of tinned or bottled fizzy drink from the Cash and Carry should bend no rules and keep at least the children happy – and spending!

Cleanliness and proper storage are the most important – and rigorously enforced – aspects of selling food to the public, and your controller must be aware of this. A visit paid to the hall kitchen in advance to see the state of work surfaces and china would not be considered overkill, and the helpers should be prepared to wash and wipe clean before the sale begins. If the weather is hot, arrangements must be made for milk, sandwiches and meat pies and anything containing cream to be brought to the hall in chill-boxes.

Basic common sense would seem to dictate the needs of the happy band in the kitchen, but the following memory-jogging list may be of some use:

| Tea | Coffee | Orange squash |
| Sugar | Milk | Biscuits |
| Crisps | Cola | Wrapped chocolate |
| Spoons | Paper bags |   biscuits |
| Tongs | Clingfilm | Kitchen paper |
| Apron(s) | Tea towels | Rubber gloves |
| Dish cloth | Kettles or tea urn | Washing-up liquid |

## General Points

There are two general requests you might make of your helpers and controllers before you finish your part of the committee meeting: first, for a few useful items that might well be forgotten. Ask them to consider bringing:

* Margarine tubs or similar to use as cash boxes
* Tape measure, ballpoint or felt-tipped pen, scissors
* Carrier-bags – customers never have enough and you may decide to announce a 'fifty pence a carrier-bagful' sale at the end
* Some helpers – as long as they introduce them personally. But that's another story. . . .

Second, and for their own benefit, you can wind up with a strong recommendation towards simplicity of dress when attending the layout and sale. No expensive coats that might be stolen or sold in error, no ornate jewellery that might catch and have the stones pulled out, or gold watches with uncertain clasps; and no handbags stuffed full of notes, bank books and credit cards – after all, it's not a shopping spree in Harrods!

# CHAPTER SIX

## *Attention all Jumble-bugs!*

With the best will in the world, no jumble sale repays the effort without adequate advertising, and this amounts to more than sticking up a few posters – though posters will play a major part in the campaign to let as many people as possible know the important details of 'where' and 'when'. Potential customers must have the information aimed at them from all sides; they must read it in the local papers and the parish magazine, see it pinned up on the notice-boards of shops, schools and works canteens and hear it promoted by word of mouth at other events.

### Planning

Advertising begins the moment the organiser enters the jumble sale date and time in the community diary, and continues with the choice of controller of advertising, to whom this chapter is addressed.

Sir or Madam, your duties commence much in advance of the others'. To start with, as long before the event as possible you must collect all the free papers that arrive on the door-mat – these may include your town's 'Leisure News', a community school newsletter and the parish magazine – and take note of their frequency, for it would be foolish to put an ad. in a quarterly paper that doesn't come out until a month after the sale.

Plan to place an advertisement (or a diary note) in *every* paper where this facility is free, and of the ones that charge, try to balance cost against the paper's circulation and whether there is an issue nicely timed for just before your sale. The thin advertising papers rely on snippets of local information to ensure their product doesn't go from doorstep to bin in one easy movement, so if they want a fee to include your piece, suggest they take a charitable attitude and waive the cost this time; it may work.

A much weightier prospect is the local paper, whose high cost per entry means that only town jumble sales may find it lucrative to advertise in this way. At around £12 for a single-column, boxed ad. three centimetres deep (often minimum size) you would have to be sure of it attracting at least twelve people who could be guaranteed to spend a pound each, just to break even; and the further out of town you are situated, the less likely that becomes. It would be safe to assume that, unless you are renowned for your fabulous sales, a three-mile limit exists outside which you might be throwing money away. But do contact the newspaper office and check their charges, and while you're at it ask about the classified 'For Sale' column where you might find an entry costs under £3 and is financially more acceptable.

When you have selected the newspaper to honour with your custom, study existing advertisements for an indication of general style; these may be found sharing a 'What's On' feature with nightclubs, cinemas, theatres, restaurants, spiritualist meetings, leisure parks, craft fairs, bingo, dance and aerobic classes, flea-markets, minimarkets, antiques fairs and car boot sales, to mention just a few. To be noticed amongst that lot, your entry must be a model of conciseness. Fancy additions like 'Super', 'Bumper' and 'Grand' only cloud the issue, for your customer wants merely to extricate the magic words 'Jumble Sale' from the mass. Mention of a Cake stall and Refreshments (unless to do so costs extra) may bring more custom, but to feature the 'White Elephant stall', 'Books' or 'the Raffle' – always assumed to be integral parts of any jumble sale – appears pathetic and inept. If your collection of books is exceptional, however, call it a 'Book Sale . . . with Jumble'.

And remember, your ad. in the paper is a net to catch those who miss the posters you dot around the area, to attract strangers who may have no idea where to find the community centre, the old people's home or the primary school, and if it doesn't contain the vital information about exact venue and time it is as useless as a mirage in the desert.

```
+------------------------------------+
| Combwick Ladies' Guild             |
| ┌────────────────────────────────┐ |
| │ JUMBLE SALE                    │ |
| └────────────────────────────────┘ |
| Friday March 10                    |
| 6 p.m.                             |
+------------------------------------+
```

```
+---------------------+    +-----------------------------+
| JUMBLE              |    |        GRAND                |
| SALE                |    |   MEMORY LANE SALE          |
|                     |    |                             |
| Goff's Hall         |    |   BARGAINS GALORE!          |
| Leyton Road,        |    | ─────────────────────────── |
|                     |    |   Popham Hall, Sunday       |
|                     |    | ─────────────────────────── |
| Sat May 7           |    | CAKES, BOOKS, TOYS          |
|                     |    | HUGE RAFFLE !!!!!           |
+---------------------+    +-----------------------------+
```

Take these three, for instance.

At first glance these advertisements look just like all the rest, but each is flawed to the extent of losing money for their cause. I'm sure Combwick Ladies' Guild considered their entry admirably short and to the point. It is fine if the only customers they want are other Combwick ladies, but anyone outside the immediate area would have to drive around looking for a queue, or a poster with the location written on it – and why should they bother when there may be a dozen other sales advertised on the same page? It should not prove too costly to include the name of the hall, plus the street where it is to be found, and this information might make an appreciable difference to profits in the long run.

Advertisement number two gives no opening time and

is simply a waste of money. This sort of mistake is generally due to an organiser casually ringing the newspaper and dredging the information he or she wants to give from memory, and it happens very often. Always write down your advertisement, even if you are booking your space over the telephone, and try to look at it from a customer's point of view. Always keep your neatly written advertisement as some slight proof that you gave the newspaper all the information, for it may be they who get it wrong!

The third advertisement was put together by someone who is squeamish at the idea of using the words 'jumble sale' and hopes to make his or her mark as an amateur blurb-writer by finding a different approach to catch the eye. Possibly it will – but in this instance it lacks the vital necessity . . . clarity! Almost every eye scanning the page on which this ad. appears *has* to reject most of what it sees, because there are usually too many desirable activities on offer that coincide or overlap, demanding that choices be made between them – an uncomfortable mental exercise disliked by many people. If any advertisement does not express its main purpose with sparkling clarity it will be quickly, and gratefully, overlooked. The searcher for jumble sales might initially be drawn by the aggressive and insistent use of capitals and exclamation marks – but as the words they form don't fit any traditional, specific and recognisable invitation, the searcher will assume it is not what he or she is looking for and ignore it.

The customers most likely to turn up as a result of this advertisement will quite possibly think they are attending an antiques fair or a market with both cheapjack and junk stall traders and may be somewhat disgruntled to find it a jumble sale, an event which from pure snobbery they normally shun; they would far rather spend £1 on an item at a market or car boot sale than do as the seller did and buy it for tenpence at a jumble! Unfortunately, every aspect of the ad., from the style the author thought stunningly dynamic to the information it omits, reinforces the idea of a commercial event. Even the timing is misleading, for Sunday is rarely considered suitable for jumble sales, while the recent growth of semi-amateur merchantry in car parks and fields across the land on this previously sacrosanct day is common knowledge. The lack of an opening time, merely forgotten by an author carried away by a masterful composition, sets a seal on the illusion, for whoever heard of a jumble without a starting time?

The simple rules of advertising any local event in any medium are: who – actually a legal requirement; what – only easily recognised, traditional definitions, please; where – as much information as is necessary and affordable; when – date *and* time. And make sure you send in your 'copy' well before the deadline, thus giving the typesetters time to get it right.

Now that you have composed the ideal notice, it seems a shame to use it just once when a copy sent to local radio stations – commercial *and* BBC – might result in its content being read over the air, thus reaching a large and valuable group of people who don't necessarily read the local papers. One stipulation these stations all make, however, is that they have the notice in writing, and it is only polite to send or hand it in with a covering letter, preferably addressed to the appropriate person rather than 'to whom it may concern'. If no one in your group is an avid listener who can furnish you with a presenter's name, look up the telephone number of the station (in the *Yellow Pages* under 'Radio Broadcasters' or 'Broadcasting Organisations'), and you will find that whoever answers your call will be only too happy to help and not at all put out or surprised by your enquiry. A little trouble taken over this small courtesy may mean your notice has a better chance than others of being read out in the 'What's On' slot when the presenter has more letters than he or she has time to air.

Local television companies may have a similar facility, although this is generally restricted to a few minutes on Friday evenings, so competition is much greater; but if you are willing to gamble the cost of a stamp and do happen to be lucky, the fact that you've been advertised 'on telly' could bring in a lot of extra custom.

Most broadcasting organisations ask for your copy at least a week in advance, while BBC local radio, if given a fortnight's notice, will send your information to adjacent stations, offering useful extra coverage if your town or village happens to be in the transmitting overlap. None of the BBC or, to my current knowledge, the commercial stations charge worthwhile causes for this service, which gives the best of free advertising and is too good to be missed.

A woefully under-used advertising facility can be the electronic information display boards that are springing up in town centres everywhere. They seem to be greeted with curiosity and general approval, but when it comes to thinking of them as superior posters with huge potential, the fundraising fraternity is proving particularly obtuse. These large, eye-catching boards run a daily program of advertisements which move across the screen and which, by virtue of their size and crisply formed, bright letters, look far more professional and authoritative than any ad. that you are likely to pin up in the area. Yet it seems that town councils are finding it hard to fill the daily requirement of around fifty-three notices per computer program, even though for charitable or fundraising groups they may do it for nothing, bless their hearts! As this innovative amenity doesn't fall neatly into any one category, its jurisdiction may be held by the secretarial and legal division, the executive office or the department of leisure and recreation, depending on the whim of the council, so contact by phone may be difficult; but walk into the reception hall of your council offices and you will find piles of message request forms just begging to be used, and a receptionist with orders to be exceptionally helpful towards anyone who expresses an interest in them.

If your council hasn't caught up with the second half of the twentieth century and has yet to provide an electronic display board, perhaps your post office has been recently overhauled and has a long, thin mini-version over the counter with space in its program for the odd jumble sale ad? You can but ask.

## Posters

Now to preparing posters, a job *previously* reserved for the 'artistic' member of the group who soon found that the task required more of a dogged, conveyor-belt technique than aesthetic whim. The first piece of work would be beautifully drawn and embellished, the second less so, the third would show signs of haste and so on until the last few, bald in their statement of fact, displayed the artist's fatigue and boredom.

Not any more! The smart controller of advertising makes it his or her first job to find out if anyone in the group has free access to a photocopier, what sizes it prints and whether they can be reduced; the second job is to work out how many copies of various sizes will be needed. To this end, think of notice-boards in shops, places of work such as factories and offices, colleges (particularly good for custom), doctors' and dentists' surgeries, hospital waiting rooms, hairdressers, pubs and the library – the mobile library for villages. Don't forget village notice-boards for three or four miles around, the church notice-boards and the one in the hall where the sale is to be held. Make a note of fences and gates belonging to supporters of the cause who wouldn't mind pinning up a good, big poster and think of others who might display small ones in their car rear windows for mobile publicity. You may be astonished to find that you can reasonably make use of thirty or more posters of differing sizes, a daunting prospect for one artist but a piffling trifle for a photocopier; and if no one you know will admit access to such a machine it is probably easier to throw yourself on the mercy of local businesses, to grovel and beg for them to run off a few free copies, than it is to sit down and draw them all yourself. Concerns that offer a photocopying service will tend to be scrupulous in their counting and you will get not one copy more than the minimum, but in an office where the photocopier is just another tool like the typewriter, somebody will blithely run off as many as you like and probably a few more for luck.

What you have to provide is one clean, neatly drawn poster in the largest size you think you will need – which tends to be A3, a size that suits most photocopiers. Commercial artists never produce artwork smaller than the anticipated printed result because any flaws or mistakes are highlighted by enlargement – in fact very often work will be drawn at twice the size so that lines are fined down and become more delicate when reduced in size. There is no reason why your approach to posters should not be just as professional.

## How to Design

First consider what you want to say, then rough it out on a piece of spare paper, remembering that as you are only producing one piece of finished artwork it should be effective in all its forms! Your first thought must be for the potential customer passing by in a bus or car so the basic information must be easy to see and quick to grasp: *what, where* and *when*. But your poster also needs to fight for attention on a crowded notice-board so other inducements and embellishments can surround the larger, more important information.

The words 'JUMBLE SALE' should be the largest on the paper and in prime position one third of the way down; the day, date, time and name of the hall should appear immediately below, and the whole message writ large enough to be taken in at a single glance from a distance. Above this group it is usual to have the name of your club or charity, while below it can go street directions and extra-tempting features of the sale, all in much smaller lettering, with any illustrations you feel may be appropriate. These proportions will suggest a portrait (tall) poster and you will probably find that most of the gaps on noticeboards are that shape, but there is nothing against using your paper the other way round, landscape (wide), if you want to be different.

Once you have decided on your wording and its sequence, it is very tempting to dive straight in and begin drawing freehand. This is not a good idea, for great care must be taken to avoid the errors of positioning attendant on rash beginnings. Who hasn't smiled in contempt at the poster that begins with plump, relaxed lettering that gets thinner and more neurotic once the artist has realised the lack of space? It can become so narrow and crowded that the 'L' of 'SALE' looks as if it is keeping a positively anorexic 'E' from plunging off the edge! A single example of such amateurism may be pinned up and forgotten, but imagine thirty copies rolling off the photocopier, the sight of each one making its creator wince.

So prepare your paper as a professional artist does. Use a soft pencil with a mark that can easily be erased and lightly rule a border all round (merely as a guide) – an inch should be sufficient at the sides, a little more top and bottom. If this is the point where you sit and look at your beautifully prepared white sheet of paper and wonder fearfully how or where you begin making bold and meaningful marks on its pristine loveliness . . . you don't; instead, try making a 'mock-up' out of newspaper headlines, rather in the manner of a ransom note – using strips of writing irrespective of what the words say. This will give you the general effect of positioning and letter size, and you can move your strips of newspaper up and down, change them around or cut larger or smaller ones until you are pleased with the result. Lightly attaching them with Blu-Tack will keep them in place and allow you to pin up the poster and survey it from the other side of the room. Now, using your ruler, make tiny pencil marks in the margin on either side to indicate top and bottom of each row of words, discard your strips and, having first taken measurements from one end of your paper to make sure they will be level, draw soft lines across; finish preparations with a carefully drawn line down the middle and make ready to sketch in your letters – starting from the centre!

Divide by two the number of letters in each line (including one for each space between words) and begin lightly sketching the two middle letters either side of the centre – or the letter that sits on the centre line if there is an odd number. Carry on, working out towards the sides, standing back occasionally to check that the letters are evenly spaced and roughly the same size (all touching their containing lines, top and bottom). Don't worry if the two outside letters overlap the margins you have drawn; as long as they don't actually touch the edge of the paper and are the same on both sides the result should be good. There is no need to copy a formal typeface in all its meticulous detail as jolly lettering of no particular style is very well suited to the subject. Your large, important information should be written in outline (see illustration) and the rest in single-line printing.

When you are happy with your pencilled result, and have *checked the spelling* (unlike the Salvation Army artist who put out a large fluorescent pink notice advertising a 'HUGH JUMBLE SALE', perhaps immortalising a lover in a way for which he might not care), rub out any unnecessary pencil marks, for to do so later may smudge the ink and ruin the poster. The final move in this part of the operation is to go over your sketch in good, thick, black felt-tip marker pen and leave to dry.

Now to the photocopier and all those copies – some of which will be the original size (A3), others half that (A4, the size of typing paper); with luck, and given a good machine operator, you will also have plenty of small ones, fitted two to a sheet of A4 (or four to a sheet of A3 if you are being charged per sheet!). All that now remains, barring distribution, is to fill in the outlined letters and illustrations with bright, *permanent* colours that won't run in the rain – a satisfying and sociable job for a few friends round the kitchen table. Or you could keep the colouring of the smallest posters for a children's art competition, selling the 'blanks' at ten pence a time at play schools, primary schools or children's clubs, or in the local shops, and offering prizes to be awarded at the end of the jumble sale – a ploy that should bring along plenty of fond mums, dads and grannies.

## Poster Distribution

By all means hand over this time- and petrol-consuming job to other members of the group who may be in a

---

*Poster mock-up with annotations:*

|  |  |
|---|---|
| Ribsthorpe Boys'Club | 20 letters upper/lowercase |
| JUMBLE SALE | 11 CAPITALS |
| AT. JUNE 18th | 14 Most Caps |
| 2·30pm | 7 |
| OAKFIELD HALL | 13 CAPS |
| HOGARTH LANE | 12 CAPS |
| Raffle·Books·Cakes·Toys | 23 l.c. |
| Admission 10p | 13 l.c. |

*Final poster:*

Ribsthorpe Boys' Club

**JUMBLE SALE**

**SAT. JUNE 18th**

**2·30 pm**

**OAKFIELD HALL**

HOGARTH LANE

Raffle · Books · Cakes · Toys

Admission 10p

45

position to visit a certain village or to ask a particular shopkeeper if he would be so kind, etc., but *do* specify where you want the notices posted so there are no gaps in coverage, and tell your helpers the date by which you want all notices on show – too early and people forget they are there or they become torn and faded, too late and they are missed by potential customers; ten days before the sale is usually a good time. And be sure to ask your helpers to remove the posters soon after the sale; out-of-date information hanging around looking untidy reflects so badly on your group.

## On the Spot

Now to the day of the sale itself and advertising in the immediate vicinity of the hall. At its boldest this can take the form of a huge banner draped across the building's fascia or at the nearest point where a lot of people may be passing; otherwise make use of a free-standing sandwich board outside the hall with, perhaps, directional arrows on each street corner from the nearest main road. Your organiser should already have ascertained whether such items can be hired from the hall, but if they can't it may be a shrewd move to have a handy member of the group make up a set of re-usable notices. The arrows need only be shaped hardboard, either nailed to a small stake to push in the bank or verge or with strings to tie them to trees and fences, and are particularly useful if your village venue is rather tucked away; the free-standing sandwich board involves very basic carpentry skills and should cost

*'The new vicar is very supportive!'*

46

only a few pounds in materials – less, if everybody involved hunts through their garden sheds and workshops for remnants of hardboard and rough wood for the frames. The trick is to cover the signs with blackboard paint, so, with the only *permanent* words being 'JUMBLE SALE' in white on the black, all that is needed on the day is to add in chalk the time of the opening of the sale, a simple message which has considerable impact and can easily be rubbed off. Any other information is superfluous; the name of the club or charity has been well advertised elsewhere and there will, no doubt, be a poster with all the details quite close to hand anyway; the arrows point to the hall, and no organisers in their right mind would stand a notice outside St John's if the sale is to be at St Luke's! And as the public assumes such sandwich boards refer to that day only, the date isn't necessary, either.

The permanent letters on arrows and sandwich board *could* be carefully drawn and laboriously painted in white gloss. Or you could cut them out of sticky-backed Fablon bought by the metre from a hardware shop. Best of all, buy ready-cut, stick-on plastic letters from an art shop – neat, professional, long-lasting and cheaper than you would imagine. And if your group are a sociable lot, you can attach by hooks to either side of the top of the sandwich board other black boards printed with 'Dance', Bingo', 'Whist Drive', 'Disco' – any activity you indulge in often enough to warrant its own permanent notice – until you become the envy of every other group around; at which point you rent out your smart notices and recoup your original costs, with interest!

Last of all, but in some country areas probably most important, do not underestimate the power of word of mouth. Plot every local event between now and your sale and make sure someone at each one stands up and spreads the word. Be it gymkhana, WI meeting, horticultural club, historical society outing to a stately home or amateur dramatics club presentation, a request to advertise a jumble sale is rarely turned down. Speak to local individuals, call in favours, make them feel that their absence will be noticed and frowned upon; appeal to better natures and issue dark threats to those of your number who enjoy the amenities you provide from your fundraising, but who don't lift a finger to help. Whether they come out of flattery or guilt is all the same; once inside the doors their purses are *yours*.

# CHAPTER SEVEN

## Is it Legal?

For many years the blithe maxim of the charity fundraising world has been *caveat emptor*, or buyer beware – so generally accepted is it that normally honourable people will unthinkingly and unashamedly lie through their teeth to make a sale, whilst the general public, having gone out for something for nothing and found that they've been had, tend to cut their losses with a rueful smile and a shrug of the shoulders. If the fudge from the fête tastes awful, who would dream of taking it back? And if the plate for which you paid fifty pence at a jumble sale is, on inspection, more Melamine than Minton, are you the person to demand a return of forty-five pence? . . . Well, it isn't worth making a fool of yourself for a few pennies and you certainly wouldn't want to appear mean. But when you buy something in a shop or from a market stall you quite rightly expect redress if it turns out to be poor value for money, broken or inedible: and when you hear of toys for sale that choke, poison or come apart to reveal lethal spikes, of exploding hairdriers and cookers that electrocute, of vermin-infested food and filthy methods of preparation, then you are wholly justified in expressing outrage. The cry goes up 'There ought to be a law against it', and laws *have* been brought in to deal with most bad practices.

The public first learns of them through newspaper reports written by journalists, who work to the rule that the only news is bad news and search out the negative aspects of each new Bill; thus it has been that those involved with fundraising have first heard that they are – supposedly – no longer allowed to sell electrical goods, home-made toys, jams and pickles, cakes and pies or to serve refreshments. But journalists rarely have room to write the entire story, and even if they had they haven't the time or training to read and understand the complexities of a Bill, itself many pages long, that is an amendment of an Act some years old that replaced an even earlier, outmoded Act. Take the Food Safety Act 1990, for instance; its origins can be traced back to a law passed in the 1870s, at a time when it was common practice for unscrupulous traders to bulk out expensive commodities with cheaper additives. Fine white wheat flour would so often be found to contain chalk or lime that cookbooks of the time advised on how to test for such contaminants, while the much prized spice, cinnamon, was often sold laced with deadly red lead, which looked the same but was a lot cheaper to produce.

Government legislation over the years has meant it is now generally accepted that if a supermarket-bought sausage roll, fish and chips from the corner shop or a ham salad from the works canteen have us teetering between life and death, then somebody can be brought to book for our dangerous discomfort. The latest Act seems to aim to make sure that processors of food of all kinds, from huge factories to tiny cafés, never bring us to such a parlous state; that their buildings and equipment are spotless before the impeccable raw ingredients cross the threshold, that everything is handled and stored in exactly the right way and that nothing can go wrong between then and the time the food enters the hands of the customer. With an Act so complex and wide-ranging, one can hardly expect a postscript saying 'none of this applies to charity fundraising, the organisers of which can poison people with impunity'.

However, enmeshed within the convoluted legal jargon is the faint hint that Mrs Jones doesn't have to have her kitchen licensed by the local authority before she can bake a cake to sell at the jumble sale, that Mrs Brown won't have to buy a new gas-stove because an official thinks hers too likely to hold germs that might be passed on to the public in her delicious quiches, and an expensively hired refrigerated van will not be required to carry these comestibles to the hall – even if that is what the press scare stories would have us believe.

A spokesperson from the Department of Health writes:

Food supplied at fund-raising and social events is in fact already covered by the law, namely, Section 10 of the Food Act, 1984, whether or not it is eaten on the premises. Under Section 10 a supplier of food at these events can already be held accountable if he or she supplies unfit food. These provisions have been carried over to Clause 2 of the Food Safety Bill [now Section 2 of the Act], so that food supplied at charitable and social events can continue to be covered. However, as the voluntary sector is already operating under these provisions, there is no reason why it should not continue to do so. I should like to reassure you that it is not the Government's intention to impose any additional responsibility in this respect.

It may come as a surprise to all the cake-makers and tea ladies in the fundraising world to find they have been operating under anything but their own whim and fancy, and a surprise to the D.o.H. spokesperson to learn that when organisers plead for a contribution to the Cake stall they rarely stipulate the letter of the law in the manufacture of the donation – in fact they don't give it a thought. But extract the essence of the Food Act 1984 (to be replaced by the Food Safety Act 1990) mentioned above, and even earlier legislation, like the Food Hygiene (General) Regulations, 1970, and it is evident that for years there has been a disregard for the law on a monumental scale. Perhaps it hasn't mattered so much in the past, when a 'tummy upset' was something to be shrugged off as an unpleasant, occasional occurrence; but at a time of food scares and a general feeling that blame must be attributed for anything untoward that can happen to anyone, can it be long before someone brings a civil court claim? Mrs White and the organiser of the church jumble sale could both be brought to law if the former's sausage rolls put a litigiously inclined person into hospital – but how often do organisers consider the conditions under which the food made at their request is prepared, stored, transported to the point of sale and then displayed? And do they even realise that responsibility rests mainly on them, *by law*?

And that is merely in respect of food (general guidelines on hygiene and storage are on pages 55–6). There are laws that cover most aspects of the jumble sale, many of them only applicable if the group raising money is carrying on a 'trade' or acting in the course of a 'business'. Before you airily assume that that couldn't possibly apply to you, it must be pointed out that certain activities of both Oxfam and the Women's Institute or perhaps even your village cricket club fall within legal definitions of the terms 'trade' and 'business'. A fundraising group might, therefore, be considered to engage in a trade or business regardless of whether it operates for profit, and regardless of whether it forms a company. There are monetary benefits in a club or society becoming a company but you, as its fundraising organiser, must be advised of the possibly less beneficial aspects. Do investigate this point as soon as possible; it may also have a bearing on other events such as dances, bingo evenings and fêtes.

One story that raised a furore in the papers concerned restrictions on the Women's Institute sale of jams and pickles – seemingly a blow to the very heart of traditional Britain. Part of the reason for it was that, like any other food-producing business regularly selling to the public, the WI is required to standardise its jars and labels and list the weight and contents – an extra chore which takes time and whittles away the profits. The next blow from bureaucracy was aimed below the belts of both the WI and the hospice movement, for it seemed that those producing hand-made toys for sale, or those selling them, would have to go about the tedious, and expensive, business of having them tested to ensure that they comply with the new safety standard, once again a law enforced on a business, or anyone deemed to be trading.

There are various criteria which local authorities would need to bear in mind before deciding who, of those people manufacturing anything at home for sale to the public, is 'deemed to be in trade'. Amongst other things (such as the profit made by the manufacturer, or a seller for private gain) the Trading Standards Department of the Somerset County Council takes the view that 'exposing food for supply more than six times in any twelve-month period would constitute trading activity'. Toymakers are liable to similar considerations, and any group selling toys *on a regular basis* should stock only those bearing the new 'C.E. mark'.

On the whole, Trading Standards officers are preoccupied with the dirty tricks of those who con the public with 'malice aforethought' and they do not rate jumble sales very high on their list of priorities; but they could, technically, pay your event a visit and close it down if they don't like what they find. If your group has any connection with the local hall – perhaps you use it as a weekly meeting place and as such are entitled to have a member on the committee that runs the hall – then it might be suggested

'*He wants to see the white elephant . . .*'

that, for the benefit of all concerned, the Trading Standards Department is asked for its guidelines on the safety of goods sold at jumble sales and for charity. Other useful people to contact, if you consider that any new legislation needs investigation and explanation, are your County Community Council and a national group called ACRE – Action with Communities in Rural England.

Meanwhile, according to a leaflet regarding the 'Safety of Goods sold at Jumble Sales and for Charity' prepared by Somerset County Council, here are a few indications of the type of materials you cannot sell. Other Councils will have their own lists.

## Electrical Equipment

It is no longer permissible to sell anything sporting the old-style red, green and black wires. However, an appliance thus wired may be of interest as a classic piece – perhaps an elegant old valve radio, or a 1950s toaster – and you are allowed to offer such an item to a dealer or collector; but cut off the wire close to the body of the classic appliance before offering it for sale, and sell it as a curio or ornament only.

Modern appliances (with green and yellow earth wire, blue neutral wire and brown live wire) should first be examined by a qualified electrician. Even so it is wise to advise the potential buyer that the appliance is second-hand and that you can give no guarantee; never claim that an article is brand new.

Discard immediately any electric fire that has no guard,

a bent guard or one which makes it possible for fingers to touch the element.

Avoid electric blankets like the plague. However, if one arrives that is pretty and fluffy and tempting, check with your Trading Standards officer – in some areas they offer free testing of electric blankets; but even if it passes all the tests with flying colours, it must not be offered to the general public without a label detailing its correct use.

Spin driers must have a safety mechanism that locks the lid until the drum has stopped spinning.

## Gas Appliances

There are two sorts of gas fire that you may be given for your sale: the sort that is fitted into a fireplace and the portable unit on wheels. They should both be checked by an expert and anyone purchasing the former should be advised to have it professionally fitted.

## Oil Lamps and Heaters

It is unlikely that you should find yourself with an antique lamp to sell, and if you do, take it to a dealer or put it into an auction. But you probably are not aware that if you offer an oil lamp for sale to the public it must have passed tests for stability, safety on overturning, smoke emission or guttering in a draught; it should be difficult to break, its fuel chamber should not leak in any position or be subject to distortion and it must bear a label stating: 'Warning: use only paraffin.'

52

Very old oil heaters can be so dangerous that it is not worth the few pennies you are likely to get for them to have possible accidents on your conscience. Modern ones are safer, but must carry the manufacturer's label that warns against use of petrol, carrying or filling when alight and using in a draughty or unventilated place.

## Carrycot Stands

These articles don't flash warning bells in the minds of those not directly connected with small children, but the rules are very strict. The stand must be strong, stable, with a retaining rail at least three inches deep, the top of which must be no more than seventeen inches from the floor. It must also be labelled with the maximum measurements for the carrycot it is designed to carry.

## Toys

It is simply a matter of common sense and adult responsibility that all second-hand toys should be vetted before being allowed on the trestle, and that any dangerous or badly broken items should be discarded where they can't be found by sharp little eyes and quick fingers. However, what is little known is that any new toys made for you to sell, or as a prize in a lottery or other game, must comply with standards first laid down in the 1970s and recently updated.

Stuffed toys *must* be made of non-flammable material – which doesn't mean that those kind and industrious people who spend their evenings beavering away – *not as a business* – with sewing needle or knitting pin for your benefit should be faced with any great expense; they can continue recycling clean material or yarn from other sources as long as they first test a tiny piece with a lighted match, and use only those that do not flare up or melt into a sticky mass. As for the stuffing, most fabric shops stock only the recommended washable, fire-retardant polyester filler that carries a British Standard Safety number, and is not at all costly.

If you are faced with the problem of a toymaker who habitually uses unhygenic old nylons or cut-up pieces of material as stuffing – easy to tell from the lumpy feel of the toy – explain that you've just found out about the regulations and supply a bag of safe filler out of funds. The improved look of the finished cuddly animal should soon bring in enough extra pennies to cover your outlay, whilst your toymaker will probably enjoy working with an easier-to-handle medium.

Wooden toys always look expensive yet steeped in nostalgia, so you are lucky indeed if you have someone (again, on an amateur basis) willing to craft trains or jigsaws for you. However, you must check that spikes are not used in the construction, nor in the decoration any lead-based paints or dyes that come off on the hands.

Anything attached to a toy that could possibly be pulled off and swallowed must be tested with a good, hard tug (officially glass eyes, plastic noses, buttons, etc., should be able to withstand a pull of approximately twenty pounds).

## The Production of Food for Sale

Having ascertained that you are, after all, allowed to sell food does not mean you can afford to be complacent for, as organiser, it is incumbent on you to ensure that such food is wholesome, uncontaminated and free of foreign bodies. This is bound to be the thought furthest from your mind when you are engaged in begging reluctant cooks to bake cakes and pies for your sale – a difficult enough job without having to insult them by asking whether they are clean in their habits!

But, be honest, aren't there always a few offerings that, knowing where they come from, you wouldn't touch with a six-foot cake fork? And should you really watch poor innocents bearing them off as a tea-time treat and think only 'what the eye doesn't see . . .'? Even the most experienced cook needs a refresher course once in a while; perhaps it is time you invited a speaker on the subject 'Cooking to Sell' for one of your group evenings. At least you will be able to say, hand on heart, that you did your best to ensure that the food on your trestles came from hygienic kitchens.

If yours is not the sort of club or group that gathers regularly to be lectured, try applying to your local Health Education Authority or Environmental Health Office for one of their excellent and up-to-date booklets containing the latest information for food producers and sellers, and ask for it in great enough numbers to be able to hand out one to each of your prospective cooks. You can give an apologetic, yet amused and conspiratorial little smile and tell a slightly twisted version of the truth: 'Of course, everyone knows that you're the *last* person to need it, Mrs Green, but you know the law today – and it really is best to stay on the right side, don't you think? What with people suing so readily and all that. . . . I would be most obliged if you would just spend a minute or two . . . it's a surprisingly interesting little book. . . . You will? Thank you, I knew I could count on you.' The law is not that she reads the booklet, but that she puts into practice its advice. You will have to hope that she recognises that some of her usual cooking procedures in the past have left something to be desired – as do those of the person of my acquaintance who likes to demonstrate her rather eccentric way of separating eggs. She breaks them into her cupped hands and allows the whites to trickle through her fingers. Unfortunately, throughout the process those fingers remain encrusted with heavy, ornate and unwashed rings. Then there's the classic comment from one lady to another overheard on a bus: 'Isn't it wonderful how clean your hands are after you've made pastry?'

The Food Safety Act 1990 makes provision for Ministers to introduce new regulations over a period of time, so any specific information written here may well be out-of-date before the ink is dry. For instance, prior to this Act coming into force government guidelines on temperature control stated that dishes containing meat, fish and dairy products must spend no more than an hour and a half between the temperature of 10°C and 63°C whilst cooling, after which they must be put into a refrigerator – but this seemingly good advice is no longer sufficient; there are now, or will soon be, times and temperatures stipulated for separate foodstuffs for the stages of their production, storage and transportation. Likewise, simple reminders of cleanliness may no longer go far enough, for whilst *I* may implore you to wash all work surfaces, the government might want you to use specific chemical cleaners for this job, and if in a year's time the boffins come up with an even more effective germ-killer then this will supersede previously ordained cleaners. And you can be sure that those compiling the Act have not forgotten the charity-event cook and fundraiser; a booklet entitled *The Food Safety Act 1990 and You – A Guide for the Food Industry* (produced by Food Sense: Crown copyright 1990) states:

> Since the Act makes it an offence to *sell* any food which fails to meet safety requirements, it applies not only to major retailers but also to small restaurants and cafés and to food sales at charity fund-raising events.
>
> It is intended that the *occasional* preparation of food for organisations like charities should not be subject to a regular programme of visits by enforcement officers. Advice will be issued to enforcement officers on how to apply the Act in this area and those organising charity events may wish to contact their local Environmental Health Department for advice.

Mild as that last suggestion may seem, every government officer spoken to urges it as the *only safe action* to take, and even if you scoff at the idea that there could possibly be any danger at all in organising a Cake stall, Tombola, Produce stall or Refreshments, being able to prove you sought advice before the event may eventually be good insurance. Perhaps, as intimated, there is little likelihood of your jumble sale being closed down, but you still have to consider the customer who demands compensation after an attributable bout of food poisoning; in this case you will wish to plead 'due diligence' in your defence and anything that helps to prove that you 'took all reasonable precautions and exercised all due diligence to avoid committing the offence' will be helpful. As this is a new plea introduced by the Food Act, no one yet knows all the legal ramifications of it and I am told it may be sufficient that you supply each of your cooks with a copy of the government's 'Ten Golden Rules' that are printed at the back of all their leaflets concerning food – but I shouldn't bank on it!

## Food Hygiene – Ten Golden Rules

1 Always wash your hands before handling food and after using the toilet.

2 Tell your boss at once of any skin, nose, throat or bowel trouble.

3 Ensure cuts and sores are covered with waterproof dressings.

4 Keep yourself clean and wear clean clothing.

5 Do not smoke in a food room. It is illegal and dangerous. Never cough or sneeze over food.

6 Clean as you go. Keep all equipment and surfaces clean.

7 Prepare raw and cooked food in separate areas. Keep food covered and either refrigerated or piping hot.

8 Keep your hands off food as far as possible.

9 Ensure waste food is disposed of properly. Keep the lid on the dustbin and wash your hands after putting waste in it.

10 Tell your supervisor if you cannot follow the rules.

*DO NOT BREAK THE LAW.*

However, there are one or two practices peculiar to jumble sales that are hardly likely to gain much prominence in an advisory leaflet, yet may mistakenly be taken for granted by an organiser as immovable tradition. For instance, when your door-to-door collecting team ask for jumble, do they tag on a plea for 'something for the Produce stall'? This ill-timed request forms a link in the mind of the householder who, having filled a bag with old and unwanted clothes and bric-à-brac, then sees nothing wrong in rummaging at the back of the larder for old and unwanted foodstuffs – possibly blown or rusted tins and out-of-date, torn or damp-affected packets. But what you really want to sell on your stall, or offer as Tombola prizes, are goods in tip-top condition, and the way to obtain these is to ask your local grocer to install a cardboard box near his checkout with an eye-catching request for donations; the customers buy extra items from the grocer's shelves – keeping him happy – and leave them in the box, making you very happy indeed when you come to collect just before the sale! Certain advice may not get through to that friend of a friend who has promised something for the Cake stall and, through lack of time, whips a quiche out of the freezer as a most acceptable and perfectly wholesome contribution; but if the buyer of this tasty savoury innocently refreezes it, the ground is carefully laid for someone to suffer a nasty bout of food poisoning. A wise organiser will study an up-to-date guide to catering practices and impress on her cooks those snippets of information that have a particular bearing on the rather odd jumble sale situation. Unless told otherwise, your happy-go-lucky band of largely untutored, occasional caterers may – in the way of all human nature – assume that certain rules don't apply to them; Mrs Walker may well understand that food should be covered, but if her triumph of a cake is iced with elaborate peaks and whirls she might consider that keeping her confection undamaged by lids or wrappings is far more important than any silly law. Miss James might think that, as she lives only a few doors away from the hall, no one is likely to catch her carrying her exposed offering along the street, and Mrs Briggs, whilst whole-heartedly in favour of animals and pests being kept away from food preparation areas, may have a blind spot over her own dear Tiddles, because 'he's almost human, and one of the family'; and even if she bars Tiddles from the kitchen it may not occur to her that the back of the car where Fido likes to travel is not a good, clean place to carry twenty assorted jam tarts and a swiss roll, all on an uncovered tea tray!

You can't get around the rules by charging a hefty admission fee then offering a free cup of coffee and a cake. The Food Safety Act 1990 (Section 2) treats, as if it had been offered for sale:

(a) . . . any food which is offered as a prize or reward or given away in connection with any entertainment to which the public are admitted, whether on payment of money or not . . .

(b) . . . any food which, for the purpose of advertisement or in the furtherance of any trade or business, is offered as a prize or reward or given away . . .

And, if you were considering it, don't offer a free glass of wine with every admission ticket or you'll fall foul of the licensing laws. The bright idea of running a bar as a novelty extra will involve obtaining an 'occasional permission'; application in writing must be made to the licensing justices at least a month, or to be safe, two months, before your sale and a fee (at least £4) is payable.

## Lotteries

The law makes very fine distinctions between lotteries and gaming, each having its own Act, but allows both when on the small scale likely to be found at jumble sales. However, if you plan to boost the takings by running a poker school in the kitchen and roulette in the corridor you would be wise to take further advice.

The lottery must not be the main or only reason that people attend the event – that is, you must not advertise a stupendous Raffle with small jumble sale as a side-line. (As if you would!)

A simple Raffle, Bran Tub, Tombola, Spin-a-wheel or Roll-a-penny is permitted as long as it is not for private gain. That means a football club can hold a raffle to fund new goalposts, but Mr Robinson must not raffle his golf clubs to subsidise his skiing lessons!

There are four kinds of lawful lottery that do not constitute gaming. Three them – private lotteries where the tickets are sold amongst a specific group of persons (such as the office sweepstake), societies' lotteries that involve registration and are on a far grander scale and local lotteries promoted by local authorities – are not likely to be held at jumble sales. The fourth kind is termed a 'small lottery' and the rules are simple to follow, but none the less little known.

From the money obtained by selling raffle tickets, you are allowed to deduct the cost of the books of tickets themselves and expenses incurred in buying prizes, which must not cost more than £50. You cannot offer money – be it cash, cheque or postal order – as a prize in itself, although a voucher for goods, such as £5 worth of meat from the butcher, is permissible. The tickets must be sold solely at the event – you are not allowed to offer them from door to door – and the draw must take place while the sale is in progress, and in public. As a matter of fairness, everyone should have exactly the same chance of winning, and this will not be the case where a strip of tickets is sold at a discount over single tickets. Also, if a ticket is drawn and the owner is not present, nor has left any name or address, then efforts must be made to trace that person. The winning slip and a note asking for the owner to come forward should be pinned on a prominent notice-board for a week or so, and the prize held back.

## The Venue

Turning from what you sell and how you sell it to *where* you sell it, you are advised to acquaint yourself with the fire and safety rules of the building and any limitations on activities allowed on the premises. For instance, if you are holding the sale in your own back garden and advertise it widely, the customers' vehicles parked as a consequence in a residential area may cause a road hazard involving the police, or you may be violating a bylaw. So if your venue is at all out of the ordinary, remember you have to check all the aspects that you take for granted about a registered hall.

An Entertainment Licence is only necessary for events involving music, singing or dancing and for which you charge an entrance fee. Most halls are licensed yearly, so unless you are planning a conga round the trestles in an un-licensed hall, this is one law that needn't worry you.

If there are a lot of mothers with young children in your locality, you might consider offering a crèche or children's play area as an additional (but strictly free!) draw. This is legal at present under both legislation and most local authorities' rules, subject to certain restrictions, in particular that no child is left with you for more than two hours. It is advisable that a parent be required to remain in the vicinity: if mother decides to sneak off to the grocers while her little darling is being entertained, there could be all sorts of problems with the child. In any event, you would be wise to contact the local Social Services for advice, particularly with regard to any changes to local policy as a result of the Children Act 1989. Better still, throw yourself on the mercy of the playgroup, who might supply registered child-minders for the event, along with some toys to keep the children occupied.


Finally, when you begin to apply all these rules there will be colleagues who think you are making a fuss about nothing and who will protest loudly that there was nothing wrong with the old ways. They will point out that no goods sold at jumble sales in the village hall have so far actually *killed* a customer, not even Mad Meg's raspberry jam and tuna-fish tarts (horrid though they may taste). In the face of such complacency, you will be greatly tempted to give in: it would be so easy to let everything flow along in its old, haphazard way. But if you have accepted the job of organiser you are presumably one of the ten per cent of people in any and every walk of life who have a sense of responsibility, and once you are aware of the laws that exist you will never be completely happy ignoring them. Stand your ground. Be firm and remember that *you* are where the buck stops. Having read this chapter you can recognise an illegal buck when you see one; keep it at arm's length, for it may be bigger than you imagine!

# CHAPTER EIGHT

# *The Layout*

## The Timing

Think carefully about when to start laying out. If you set the starting time too early the job will be finished long before the sale opens and you will have a roomful of bored, grumbling, waiting helpers all telling you what else they could be doing with their time. But if you underestimate the amount of jumble likely to arrive at the hall and thus start spreading it out too late, far worse will befall. Everyone will be rushing around too much to voice recriminations at first, but as more and more bulging black plastic sacks arrive and the hands of the clock sweep ever faster round its face, general panic will set in and the atmosphere will soon bristle with discontent.

None of this will be helped by the waiting customers, some of whom may have arrived an hour before the start. Quick to size up the situation from their vast experience of jumbling, they will be delighted to alleviate the dullness of queueing by offering 'helpful' raillery with every fresh load of stock carried into the hall. But their enjoyment of your predicament will lessen as the advertised time of opening approaches, and if they sense you won't be ready by then the comments will take a much nastier turn. Ten minutes late and the crowd will have become a mob, bickering amongst themselves and hostile towards the helpers – who in their turn will get upset at being treated roughly after all their hard work. Which, effectively, means one half of the community against the other, and all of them blaming you.

Try to arrange to lay out the night before a morning sale or in the morning before an afternoon one. The first major benefit will be the absence of bored and curious customers making life difficult outside the door, the second that you and your helpers have a break before the sale proper. There is still the possibility of last-minute sacks of jumble arriving the next morning or after lunch, so allow enough time to spread their contents before the doors open.

There is a traditional planning maxim for any time-consuming job: however long you think it will take, double it and add an hour! This may seem a little excessive for a jumble sale – but not much. There are two imponderables: how much stock will turn up on the day, and how many helpers will turn up to spread it out. Regarding the former, a jumble sale produces its own momentum. In addition to the collection brought in by your scavenging party, most of your helpers will arrive with some last-minute things of their own, a carrier-bagful from a neighbour and, perhaps, another from someone in the next street. You will be surprised at how many complete strangers have 'jumble looking for a sale to happen': the throwouts of a ruthless cleaning spree or the detested larger size clothes, abandoned now the slimming diet has begun to bite; more often the remnants of a sale held just before, and brought hopefully, rather in the manner of ships of toxic waste cruising the seas looking for an unwary country in which to dump their cargo.

Whilst an organiser must express eternal gratitude to the public for contributing goods to be sold (whether or not these, on closer examination, prove to be good, bad or indifferent) this does not mean that he or she is obliged to accept any old leavings of other jumbles – a firm 'no thank you' to a mass of obvious rubbish *benefits* a sale far more than does spreading it on the tables just in case someone might spend a few pennies on it. Most jumble-bugs, however vague in other situations, seem to have photographic memories for items turned over on a trestle which, if seen again months later, condemn the later sale as a poor thing that cannot amass its own, original stock. And should any of the stuff have about it the whiff of long, damp storage it will very quickly contaminate every good item it touches on your tables.

Occasionally a group may be offered a charity shop's old stock, generally a wealth of crimplene in a peculiar grey-green-brown colour and of indeterminate shape. So complacent are the organisers and helpers at having cut the job of collecting stock from door to door that it does not occur to them to unpick the sewn-on price labels bearing the shop's name. If anything, they imagine their customers will be pleased to buy a dress that cost around £40 when new, was offered for £3 by the charity shop but is now available for the incredible sum of ten pence. Their psychology is faulty! The people who attend jumble sales have rarely hit rock bottom; they are just prudent, sensible people, many of whom look upon it as a hobby and are excited by the idea that one day they may take home a stupendous bargain. Most have enormous pride – and infinite choice, for if one sale provides nothing of interest then the next one, or the one after that, might. If it becomes obvious to them that they are being offered the dregs, articles at third hand or stock others can't sell, they are as capable of feeling insulted as you are and will do exactly what you would do – walk away! And, what's more, those long memories will mean they never attend a jumble sale run by the offending group again.

There is another danger in accepting a job lot of other people's left-overs – for, while too small an amount of stock is what every organiser dreads (especially if the advertising campaign has been super-efficient), paradoxically an over-abundance of items can be the greater threat, as witnessed in a Scout hut in a small town near the Devon-Somerset border.

It was to be the biggest and best playgroup jumble sale ever, a vast collection of stock had been gathered from many sources over several months. Excitement soon grew at the layout as the two rows of trestles flanking the door and stretching to the far end of the wooden hut began to fill. Suits, coats and evening dresses were put on hangers and draped around the walls, and when there was no wall left to adorn they were hung from the low, sloping roof timbers where their trailing ends brushed the faces of the beavering helpers and became entangled in the mountains of clothes that grew ever higher and higher on the trestles. When the helpers finally took their places behind the two long rows of overladen tables they laughed to find that even the tallest of them had to stand on tip-toe to see over the top, and they chattered excitedly about all the playground equipment they would certainly be able to afford when everything had been sold. They could hardly wait to open the doors. Meanwhile, a respectable queue of around forty people had gathered outside and they were just as avid to view the Aladdin's cave within. Their initial response when the doors did open must have been gratifying – a sharp intake of breath and round-eyed amazement as they took in the scene – but very soon it all went drastically wrong.

Once the White Elephant stall had received due attention the customers turned eagerly to the clothes and grabbed in their usual manner at promising corners of material that protruded from the middle of the pile. They pulled, they tugged; they tried forcing in their hands and forearms to free the garments and then felt crushed by the weight of the pile; they wrenched shoulders, broke fingernails and snagged hangnails yanking at the heap; they took armfuls of the stuff and threw it on the floor whilst uttering imprecations not fitting in the presence of young mothers and their babes; then as waves of great weariness tinged with nausea washed over them (a state peculiar to a surfeit of jumbling, often experienced by the dedicated as they indulge in the sixth or seventh sale of the day) they walked out to breathe the sweet fresh air and blot out the memory of defeat from their minds. Some thought they knew of a better jumble and went to it, others ambled off to their gardens or the telly; a few, a very few, in grim determination tried to turn over the long heap from end to end, and did indeed find bargains – but they spent no more money than they would have had there been less for sale. A scant twenty minutes after the doors had been expectantly flung open, the disappointed organiser started adding up the takings, while her weary helpers began the loathsome job of packing away almost as much clothing as they had so recently unpacked – a chore made no easier by the news that all their effort had raised a meagre £60!

## The Style

Having arrived at the hall at, you hope, exactly the right time to begin the layout, you don't wish to waste minutes discussing how best to site the tables – or, having set them out and begun covering them with goods, to find they could have been better arranged in the first place.

The shape of the room dictates the best positioning for the trestles, some rooms being so oddly shaped that any solution must be a compromise. This can, in fact, produce a good atmosphere (rather like in war time): helpers and customers against the odds. But at the beginning of any sale the relationship between the two sides is confrontational, to say the least, and whatever shape the room the layout of tables needs to give the helpers a feeling that there is some sort of barrier between them and the crowd.

Most rooms are a simple rectangle, possibly with a stage at one end, and one of two practical – and defensive – styles is normally adopted. The more popular is probably 'Backs Against the Wall', with tables ranged around the walls, helpers behind them and customers milling around in the middle; while the other, 'Wagon Corral', has the helpers safely in the middle of a protective square of trestles, like American settlers with their wagon train round which the 'Injuns' circle. Of the former, the most useful aspect is the way in which Cakes, Raffle and Nearly New can be separated from less salubrious wares; the biggest drawback is that a good press of people will inch back the tables and pin the poor helper against the wall. The latter style has the advantage of requiring fewer helpers to run the stalls; but the snag for mature helpers is that any escape from the encirclement means undignified tunnelling underneath the trestles. If the room is big enough and there are plenty of trestles, a square of tables containing jumble in the centre with Prestige stalls and attractions along one wall makes the best of both worlds.

## The Stalls
### White Elephant

Whichever style you choose, your initial thought must be for the White Elephant stall, which will be the object of the Great Rush – so the first rule is never to site it near the door or it will cause a blockage. Second, give it as much room as possible, bearing in mind that after the first five minutes it will be so depleted that slower moving neighbouring stock can take a lot of its table space.

How to lay out general household jumble (and the accompanying Rembrandt, Cartier watch and Wedgwood tea service) depends very much on what you get and what you are allowed to sell (see Chapter Seven). An irritating but insoluble problem is that of breakages. You may have piled those plates with that pretty little cup and saucer on top in a good, safe position at the back between the pressure cooker and the box of shoe cleaning brushes, and set the delicate glasses before them, protected from the edge of the table by a tray of broken beads and make-up – well, you did your best and nobody could do better. Nothing will stop the plunge of hands that thrust and grab, often blindly as the rest of the customer's head and body can find no entry through the heaving barrier of torsos in the front row. If you have a fair selection of goodies on this stall a lot of your customers will feel there is no time to pay for each item separately, and you will be treated to the sight of teetering piles of breakables precariously clutched to bosoms by one hand as the other flails in and out, seizing this piece of china to check the maker's mark underneath, pulling that plate out from under everything else. Little wonder that items slide off clutched collections or slip from an insecure grasp to land with a crash, that heaps of china are tipped over or things fall off the edge of the table.

As a jumblophile myself, even in the thick of it I am aware that my companions and I are making a quite disgraceful display of greed and grab, but without that driving force, may it be said, jumble sales would have very few customers indeed. Better to remove the most delicate items from harm's way and display them as if they were costly, perhaps on a cloth, where they will be kept aloof from the first excitement. When the atmosphere has relaxed the customers will cross the room to look at them in a more leisurely fashion, and may be willing to pay a little more. Anything really good should be taken to a dealer beforehand (for selling or pricing), displayed on the Nearly New stall or commandeered for the Raffle.

It is better for tall or bulky items such as lawnmowers and furniture to be stood to one side rather than in front of the table, where they can throw customers off balance, especially when the pressure of other customers is applied from behind. Consider spreading these goods on the stage or, on a sunny day, outside where they can be inspected by the queue (with a helper in attendance, of course). You could even hold a mini-auction!

Boxes of bits are irresistible, but beware of putting them under the table where they are an invitation to customers to crouch down and investigate; the investigator proves as much of a hazard to the rest of the public as do the previously mentioned bulky items. And such a 'hazard' *has* been known to bite the odd leg when in claustrophobic panic at finding itself hemmed in!

To some minds, placing Household Linen alongside the predominantly household goods on the White Elephant stall is a neat continuation of one thought; to the crafty it's a good opportunity to practise salesmanship. 'Wouldn't it be a pity to break that lovely glass you've just bought – why don't you have this pillow slip to use as wrapping? Just a minute, I think there's another one somewhere . . . you might as well buy the pair. Oh, and you could wrap that bone china cup and saucer in this beautiful tablecloth; don't they go well together? There now, all safe and snug in your bag . . . that will be thirty pence for the tablecloth (it's *such* a good one, all that lace) and ten pence for each pillowcase. Thank you. Now, Mrs Jones, you'll need something to wrap round that vase. . . .'

## Toys

Another stall most lucrative for dealers, and therefore visited at a rush at the beginning, is Toys – also and understandably the target of every small child in the room. While it is wise to extract playthings from the other hardware received so that toy-seeking small children aren't damaged in the Great Rush, don't then put the Toy stall adjacent to the White Elephant and Books. Siting Toys, White Elephant and Books together makes a dealer's paradise, with everything available at an exaggerated reach and steam-rollering side-shuffle – but it doesn't make allowance for the small hopeful at the table's edge. Far better to site Toys between, say, Household Linen and Children's Clothing further round the room where the stall will be approached in a more leisurely fashion, and leave children's books to the Book stall, where a highly collectable *Rupert* or *Noddy* can be fought over by grown-ups. Yes, even children's annuals now command a high price amongst adult collectors.

Jigsaws, if obviously *well looked after*, sell well on either Book or Toy stalls. They are *most* lucrative if you take the trouble to put the pieces into a clear plastic bag within the box before putting them on sale. It is surprising how many jumble, fête and car boot sellers fail to do so when a secure package contained in an undamaged box will reassure a buyer into spending up to £1 for a thousand-piecer of good make. Plainly no one will hazard more than tenpence on a baggy-sided cardboard box from which the loose pieces may have spread far and wide, or a box bearing the legend '1 pce missing', for the investment is not just in money but in the customer's time. Sellotaping the sides as a last-minute solution does not convince; a friend of mine once bought a most tempting jigsaw of a montage of film stars' faces, one of Waddington's de-luxe range, with the lid carefully stuck down on all sides, only to find on opening it that each piece of the picture had become unstuck from the cardboard backing. A load of expensive confetti – and what a disappointment.

## Books

Now to Books, a much loved stall. There's something far more acceptable about a second-hand book than a second-hand anything else – and the stall is easier to run than most as you can stick firmly to three basic prices: for hardbacks, paperbacks and magazines, with perhaps a little licence for condition, weight and subject matter. A very large, beautifully bound and looked-after volume may cry out for a seventy-five-pence price tag, but if the subject is *Religion in Schools 1953–1969* or *The Life Cycle of the Common Bedbug* you take what you can get. The majority of your customers will favour paperbacks which, if in a clean condition, should never be sold for less than ten pence each; it is not worth displaying books that have lost their covers.

The main problem you will have on this stall is physical control of the stock, much of which will take lemming-like plunges off the edge if not 'caged'. It's a good idea to put the books into cardboard boxes – specifically the sturdy, low-sided fruit boxes already mentioned, the right size to take two rows of paperbacks with the spines free enough for a finger to pull them out without difficulty. A line of these boxes set along the edge of the stage and tilted at an angle on bricks or against the legs of chair is the ideal situation. With the books nearer the eyeline, more people can read the titles at one time, and stock thus displayed is not subject to the same press of bodies as that on the table, so is therefore less likely to fall on the floor.

One ploy to speed a quick turnover of customers is to make sure that all the titles on the spines run the same way. This saves that awkward wagging of the head and turn of the body which can double the time a person spends at your stall (but not, alas, the number of purchases). Or, far worse, they get bored and leave just before reaching all those books that might have appealed to them.

Last but not least, look out for first editions. This is not just a flippant comment; such a book is far more likely to arrive unrecognised on a jumble sale stall than is, say, a

Van Gogh painting – as Douglas Matthews, Librarian of the prestigious London Library had reason to discover when a thoughtful jumbler, recognising the Library's label, offered to return an old book picked up at a jumble sale for a mere ten pence. Mr Matthews had certainly been aware of the loss of the volume (part one of a three-part novel by Trollope) but the Library would have had to find a hefty £2,000 for a replacement set!

## Clothing

Time now to turn our attention to what will probably form the bulk of the sale stock: clothing. At first thought this would seem to be a simple matter of sorting gents', ladies' and children's garments onto their allotted tables – with the added refinement of separate areas for blouses, skirts, coats, etc. But this is not necessarily so and there are some rules that, if adhered to from the very beginning, can save a lot of problems later on.

The most common fault lies in allowing the trestles to be piled up and up – maybe not reaching the extremes mentioned earlier, but still enough to weary your customers before they have had a proper look through everything. Even if the stock is just half a metre deep, some shorter customers will still have to work with their arms outstretched at shoulder height, a position that can only be sustained by the fittest for a few minutes. Of course the problem is not that there are too many short customers, but too few trestles, and by the time you have realised that the clothing stalls need thinning out all the

other trestles are in use. A diplomatic word with the Shoe and Handbag sellers right at the beginning will save you one table if you point out that the natural setting for footwear is on the floor; neat rows of shoes by a wall, and a chair at each end for customer comfort whilst trying on, looks very well thought-out and attractive. (Handbags can be in boxes at either end; they tend to fall off tables, anyway.)

A few rules on sorting clothes in the first place will ensure that what fills the trestles has a right to be there. State firmly:

1 All *badly damaged* items must be put in boxes. Do not accept the 'someone might want it to unravel the wool' or 'but the lace is pretty' arguments. The garments will still be available for inspection on the floor at the end of the table.

2 All *smelly* items to be put in a box by the door and removed from the premises before the sale starts.

3 Garments in *good condition* to be offered to the controller of Nearly New – but his or her decision is final.

4 *Small* items like socks, gloves, scarves, handkerchieves, bras and pants should be separated into boxes. People will love to delve through them whether they are on the floor or brought up onto the table when room is available.

You must also impress on your helpers that the contents

of every bagful must be spread evenly across the trestles, ensuring a good mix of size, style and condition. This is vital if you have been conned into accepting another jumble's left-overs – which, you will remember, have already been picked over by 'professionals'; even if time *is* short, a bag of unknown content carelessly upended onto a table could form an unrelieved wall of rubbish that would kill your sale stone dead.

Should your best efforts come to naught and, even after careful weeding, large quantities of clothes remain trestle-less after the height of half a metre has been reached, consider piling the stuff in empty floor space or leaving it unsorted in the middle of the room – your customers will do the rest! In fact, they'll positively revel in it, loving nothing more than a proper 'jumble' of things to investi-gate. This raises the point of Obsessively Tidy Helper, who you will find standing at the clothes tables trying to fold and tastefully arrange the odd garments as they are sorted by the others.

She (it's usually a woman) may go unnoticed for a while, quietly standing aloof as everyone crawls around the floor getting dusty, tugging at the outspillings of sometimes unsavoury plastic bags, dibbling in the untidy mass like upturned ducks on a pond. Her self-appointed job of imposing strict order on everything may be brought to your notice by other helpers grumbling that she isn't pulling her weight. If not, the frustrations of an occupa-tion akin to emptying Loch Ness with a ladle may cause her to explode in pure anger as yet another article is thrown carelessly onto her precisely ordered territory.

Now is the time for tactful redirection onto the Cake stall or Shoes and Handbags, so that she can line them up like soldiers on parade and not ruin the jumble atmosphere; otherwise she will spend the whole sale tutting, fuming and refolding as a skirt is pulled from the bottom of a neatly aligned pile and thoughtlessly tossed aside, or a blouse is shaken out of its folds then discarded. For her the trestle becomes a battleground and the customers an irritation; who knows, *your* sale may be the one where she goes 'over the top' and refuses to let anyone near because they are nasty, untidy creatures who ruin her straight lines and pretty colour combinations!

Only slightly less fussy is Ants-in-her-Pants, who during the sale finds it impossible merely to stand behind the stall and take money. Her fault stems from not knowing how a serious jumbler works; she expects her customers to pluck an item here and there, not realising that a real jumble-bug doesn't consider a jumble truly done until every article has been inspected. To this end the serious cus-tomer (and there are bound to be several of them at every sale) will stand four square at the table's edge and work solidly and methodically in one direction. The effect on the stock will be as if a dog with sideways crab-like tendencies has been digging furiously to bury a bone, for suddenly there will be a great heap of clothes already inspected to one side of the customer, while the table in front of her will be almost bare. This hiatus Ants-in-her-Pants can't resist and she will sweep up a fat armful from the already inspected pile and plonk it down in the gap, thus keeping the level of clothes nice and even. This may make her happy, but not the jumble-bug, for whom a definite sense of *déjà vu*, even paranoia, begins to set in – especially when she turns over the same, distinctive sweater for the sixth time. Ants-in-her-Pants will continue her levelling operation until the last customer has left, and if she is sited at the confluence of two stalls, say Ladies' and Gents' Clothing, she will wear herself to a frazzle trying to keep them separate as well as evenly layered.

Without her frantic ministrations your sale will proceed perfectly satisfactorily; the clothes may surge like the tide in one direction, but there will probably be another jumbler coming the other way to counter the action, and if Gents' get mixed up with Ladies' it never seems to matter as most of your customers can tell the difference. (Mr Williams is not likely to go home with a chic little floral print frock and a puzzled frown, now is he?) At the layout it is very hard to predict who will behave in this way during the sale, but it won't hurt to point out to your assembled staff that the jumblers who are likely to buy the most will be working in methodical fashion from one end of the trestles to the other, so they should try not to impede their progress.

Obsessively Tidy and Ants-in-her-Pants have a close relative in Patronising Helper, who may come to the layout disguised as Cheerful, Willing or Good-hearted and will happily plunge elbow deep into the unsorted stock. The warning signs come when she holds up a ghastly, crushed, baggy and worn-out garment that you know for a fact she wouldn't dream of wearing, and begins to enthuse about its better qualities. Ignoring its atrocious

*'The only white elephant at this jumble sale is the chairman . . '*

67

colour that turns most complexions to sludge (including hers, and well she knows it), she will gush over how well made it is and what a flattering style for someone with big hips and a protruding bottom. You may be inclined to dismiss this with a merry quip – 'If you like it so much why not buy it yourself?'; but think ahead and tactfully 'promote' her to a Prestige stall, where she will be in her element. Madame La Jumbler is not to be patronised; she probably has more style and more exclusive labels on her clothes than Patronising Helper, who would rather go bankrupt than buy second-hand. Yet the incomes of both ladies may be similarly limited. Indeed, Madame La Jumbler may actually despise the helper for her newer but mass-produced, cheap clothing and compare it unfavourably with her own, which might be a little faded and worn but is made of the best-quality materials that age gracefully, in classic styles that never look dated; she's no fool, she can wear Jaeger, Aquascutum, Pringle, Hermès and never break the bank.

To run a Clothing stall a little knowledge of the psychology of a jumble sale can be helpful. Against most fond imaginings, nobody attends solely to support the cause; the rare person with such a pure motive just gives a donation and stays at home. A few people feel it politic to be seen spending money at the event and will honour the Prestige stalls with lavish custom before taking tea, their purchases laid conspicuously on the table before them; but they never involve themselves in the Great Rush and would shudder to think of picking over old clothes.

*Everyone else is in it for themselves.* At first, this would seem a terrible indictment of ninety per cent of your customers (and probably helpers as well), but isn't their enthusiasm and competitive drive what you need? Surely if you had decided to hold a dinner-dance instead, you would expect the money-paying revellers to enjoy themselves, not sit around the walls with cotton-wool in their ears, waving away food and drink and refusing to dance just to prove their honourable intentions towards the fund. Rid yourself of the idea that your customers should approach your event as if lining up for brimstone and treacle at Dotheboys Hall!

If the clientèle are keen to get at your trestles, they are probably old hands at jumbling who come with an ingrained set of expectations, unwritten and unspoken but reinforced by previous experience. Attendance at many other jumble sales has given them a norm to go by – even a shrewd reckoning of how much they are likely to spend overall. Most, other than dealers and car booters, if pressed would say they expected that sum to be £3 to £4, which has to include admission, raffle tickets and refreshments. When they begin to root through the gallimaufry of clothes on the trestle they will expect to pay a specific price (usually ten or twenty pence) for an average item (e.g. shirt, blouse, trousers or skirt) because that is what is most often charged; if thirty or forty pence per garment is asked some will make no comment, but others will complain bitterly, try to bargain or storm off. This has less to do with meanness than with a feeling that you've 'moved the goalposts' to spoil their enjoyment. What least impresses a customer is when, eagle eyed and triumphant, he or she finds something gorgeous, missed by the Nearly New stall's helpers so left amongst the ordinary jumble of clothes on the trestle, only to be told: 'Oh, *that's* rather nice. Cashmere, isn't it? That will have to be £1, don't you think?' No, the customer does *not* think so . . . not that it isn't worth £1 but purely because the seller is felt to be cheating, breaking the unspoken rules of the game, and any pleasure in the bargain has been spoiled.

You won't win because jumblers rarely exceed their self-imposed price limits on the jumble stalls, and if they do they will simply make fewer purchases and you'll be left with more unsold raffle tickets and teas than otherwise. However, they may consider the wares on the Prestige stalls exempt from their jumble sale budgets, and happily spend more on the understanding that a cake for Sunday tea comes out of the housekeeping money, or that toiletries to put by for Christmas presents will save money later. Curiously enough, garments on the Nearly New stall can be equally free of limitations: the very act of preselection endows them with a superiority that allows a price ticket ten times greater to go unchallenged. It may be that jumblers respect the helpers' good taste, or the time and energy put into sorting, valeting and laundering; or perhaps they are swayed by attractive presentation.

## The Prestige Stalls
### Nearly New

Returning to practicalities, the controller of Nearly New must be firm and turn away anything damaged or wildly unfashionable – not always an easy job as helpers can be oddly insistent that their choice is included on your rail.

When checking for wear and tear, particular points to watch out for are worn or dirty collars; broken stitches in the sleeve/body seam (especially at the back); holey elbows; missing buttons at bodice front, waist or cuffs; stains (particularly down the front); rotten elastic at the waist; holes (or something nasty) in the pockets; split crotch seams; worn seat or knees shown as thinning, shininess or bagginess; tears in the hem. Brand-new garments can often be distinguished by the maker's label still uncreased and stiff with dressing – but don't put any value on the presence of the plastic thingummy that once dangled the price tag; there seems to be a breed of human capable of wearing clothes with this irritating article still attached.

As you study the garment for damage, be aware of various style points. Extreme collar, sleeve and cuff shapes are a give-away, as are width of trouser bottom, style of skirt and the colour of or pattern on the material. Some items are particularly representative of an era and as such may sell to someone attending, say, a 1960s or 1970s dance, but not at a great price. However, genuine 1920s and 1930s clothes are much sought after by collectors and advice should be taken on how best to sell them. Look around your local antiques market; there may be a dealer who specialises in such things. Gentlemen's suits are always disappointing; they may be of good quality and hardly worn but will attract little interest, mainly because they tend to sit in wardrobes so long that they are vastly out of fashion when finally thrown out – and very few men will buy them to wear as 'work clothes'. Likewise, fur coats can be hard to shift now that public opinion has turned against them.

Timing is important, too. If that fur coat is to sell at all, it will obviously do best at a winter sale – just as a sundress will be most acceptable at an early summer one – but as people don't cast off their old clothes to order, the garments you receive will quite probably be wrong for the time of year. Sorting and storing everything until its appropriate season would of course be the answer, but is usually impossible, for you would need to be a fanatic with infinite patience and a large spare room. However, there is a lot to be said for creaming off a few carefully chosen articles to put by for the summer fête (cotton shorts, skirts and dresses; sunhats and filmy scarves) or for the Christmas bazaar (gloves, woollen scarves, thick coats and jumpers; glamorous party wear). Not only will these appear more desirable at the right time, but they may fetch more money when away from the jumble sale environment.

Whether to price the Nearly New items before the sale is a vexed question. One type of customer will scuttle quickly by, convinced that anything 'hung up' must be far too expensive for them. Try grabbing their attention by attaching signs proclaiming 'ALL AT £1' or even '50p EACH' – which may mean selling the goods at a low price, but still much higher than that charged on the ordinary jumble stalls, and with a faster, probably more certain, turnover.

On the other hand, scornful of such small fry, are you prepared to angle for bigger fish? Another type of customer will be automatically drawn to the good-quality Nearly New and may respond to a totally different treatment. If the goods are left tantalisingly unpriced these probably better-off customers may be prevailed upon to pay as much as the seller judges he or she can afford – giving the seller immense leeway for inspiration, intuition and daring (the price can always be dropped, as a special favour, if the customer hesitates). But be warned! With this method previous, casual acquaintance with the customer can be a two-edged sword; it *may* act as a lever to prise open the purse or wallet, but it might equally scare the customer away, feeling that any personal relationship, however slight, could cause them to spend more than they can afford. The balance has to be nicely judged and carefully executed.

Luck plays a part, of course. A whole rail of expensive, size ten clothes won't sell if all the jumblers that afternoon turn out to be hard-up and size sixteen; but if in the event just one person finds something that fits and is irresistible and doesn't blink at a high asking price, you can make more profit on the one item than the rest of the rail sold at knock-down prices. It's horses for courses! And you must try to foresee what type of customer your sale is likely to attract that day. (Will there be a handful of affluent jumblers?) Otherwise the failure of better-off organisers to understand that, unlike themselves, many people simply cannot afford to spend a few pounds on the spur of the moment can leave them with vast stocks of unsold goodies.

One of the best Nearly New stalls ever encountered, although in a humble church hall, had a sumptuously stocked rail beside a corridor, also clothes-lined, that led to a well lit ante-room equipped with a chair and cheval-glass (presumably supplied by the thoughtful saleslady). Here the female customers could try on skirts, dresses and suits that had been expertly chosen and attended to, in an atmosphere like that of a good dress shop. Care and forethought were well rewarded as the clever (and obviously experienced) lady in charge wooed and flattered her customers away from the idea that they were buying jumble, and even if they spent more than they had intended, they went home immensely pleased with their bargains.

## Games and Goodies

Other Prestige stalls such as Tombola, Produce, Toiletries or Plants are easy enough to arrange, the general rule being to make them as different and as separate from the ordinary jumble stalls as possible. The Produce stall especially must sparkle with cleanliness (see pages 55–6 for vitally important information on this subject).

## Additional Money-spinners

There is another source from which to draw income even before the sale opens: the captive audience outside the front door, waiting in the queue. A cheerful, outgoing chap can jolly the queuers into buying raffle tickets before their purses and pockets have had a chance to empty (but see pages 57–8 for legal requirements) and afterwards he can rove around selling to the latecomers as they take tea. Or how about providing those waiting with entertainment by buskers – the school band, perhaps, or a Brownie and Cub sing-song? If the hat is then taken around by an engaging small child, who can fail to throw in a few coppers? Also, at the risk of being repetitive, do remember to brief the refreshments team to arrive early. Serving tea and coffee to the queue will gain the extra custom from both those who plan to rush on to another sale the moment they've finished at your trestles, and from others who live near enough to prefer a cup in their own homes after-wards. Serving outside the hall should cease ten minutes before the sale begins and dirty cups cleared before the Great Rush.

If you want to make people stay longer, try wafting mouth-watering smells at them from the kitchen. Coffee beans heated under the grill are good for this, but best of all is toast. Suitable to be eaten in all seasons and at all times of day, with no great initial outlay or lengthy baking sessions for the sellers, a slice of buttered toast produces probably the most tempting aroma of all and, whilst still making a profit for you, will be pleasingly light on the customer's pocket. Offer brown or white, spread with a choice of butter or low-fat margarine, so that even dieters can justify taking a break. On a chilly day, add jacket potatoes and hot soup to the menu and your group could become well known for its five-star jumble sales!

71

## Decisions

Shortly before you open you will have to decide whether to allow the helpers to put by what they want from the trestles. Some organisers are firmly against this, fearing the tables will be too depleted of good stuff before the jumblers arrive; others take the more sensible view that the helpers who have done all the hard work have a good idea of what's for sale and are probably inclined to pay more in the interests of making the event as big a success as possible; moreover they *should* have first pick as a reward. Otherwise the workforce can be most unhappy, trapped in one place behind a trestle watching all the bargains being snapped up around them; for the idea that those running the sale are different from those attending it is much mistaken. Anyway, what the punters don't know about they won't miss – just as long as you hide the evidence of pre-sale bargains! Nothing riles a queue of jumblers more than reaching the White Elephant to find the best stuff already put aside as 'sold' and in full view, ranged behind the stall. Do make sure any helpers' early purchases are hidden safely and prudently away in an ante-room or other secure part of the building, or failing that in someone's car boot.

To stop the queue of jumblers watching your every move (such as helpers snaffling all those bargains before the customers are allowed in) it is handy if you have a back door that can be used by staff – who must be told to use it – so that the main door leading directly into the hall can be kept closed; but if that is not possible, please don't lock the jumblers out in the cold if you can let them stand in the foyer. Those who arrive first may be a nuisance, but they are the keenest, will wait longest and might spend the most; and there's no profit in freezing them. If the beginning of the queue is cheerful and chatty that atmosphere very often spreads backwards, with other members joining in as they arrive, but if the front dozen are cross and miserable it can cast a pall over all of them – which rarely puts anyone in the mood for frivolous spending and, in its turn, upsets the helpers who wonder why the customers are all grumpy.

This happened at one hall where there was no foyer and no back door, so the jumblers were queueing outside, coat collars turned up against the squally showers and feet stamping to ward off the chill. They were resigned to a long, cold wait but most of them had known what to expect when they set out, so what happened over the next three-quarters of an hour proved particularly galling. One by one the helpers arrived and tried the handle of the locked, blank wooden door; each then knocked and stood back to wait the minute or two it took the organiser to put down what she was doing and cross to turn the key in the sinisterly grating lock. Then this highly suspicious, beaky-nosed individual drew the door open a crack to peer accusingly at the first queue member in her limited sight, obviously convinced that he and his companions would try any fiendish trick imaginable to break into the hall before she was ready for them. Each time her gaze finally reached and recognised the helper, a reluctant 'Oh, it's you' was prised from her lips and the door held open barely wide enough for the newcomer to squeeze through, bags and all. And yet again the indignantly quivering nose and the warning, baleful glare were applied to the crack before the door was slammed shut and firmly re-locked.

As there were a lot of helpers and this pantomime was repeated for every one of them, the crowd outside the hall were exposed to such venomous scrutiny at four-minute intervals that they began to feel uneasy . . . then insulted . . . then boiling mad. But they had already invested a lot of time and discomfort in waiting for the sale to begin, not to mention having missed the start of others, so there grew a grim determination to make the best of it – but they didn't have to like it! When the time came they rushed into the hall like soldiers in a bayonet charge, and with about as much charity in their hearts. As for the organiser, one look at the thunderous faces that bore down upon her must have made it only too clear that her mistrust was well founded, and next year, sadly, she will redouble her efforts to keep the barbarians at bay. Whether anyone will bother to wait outside her door is another matter.

# CHAPTER NINE

## Thieves, Rogues and Cheeky Devils – or Dire Warnings No. 2

Without impugning the characters of your many honest and honourable customers, it has to be said that jumble sales do attract a good many rogues. It may be surprising to think that anyone should want to steal something worth only a few pennies, but perhaps that is why they do it: if it's worth so little it doesn't matter. It always comes as a shock to helpers* when they see someone stealing, because they imagine their customers to be as full of good will as they are; yet one or two may tend to feel sorry for the miscreants, mistakenly believing them to be motivated by poverty. This is rarely so. Some people make quite a business of thieving from the trestles, and a few crimes are so audacious they will leave you marvelling.

Take Mrs X and her daughter, for instance. The sale in aid of a Hertfordshire cricket club was being laid out overnight, and those members' wives dragooned to do the job began arriving at the clubhouse soon after seven. As is so often the case in an urban environment, with the cricketers drawn from a wide area, not all the lady helpers knew each other, but they soon struck up a friendly acquaintanceship and worked in cheerful harmony. One woman seemed to have an easy authority and knowledge of how to run a jumble, and it seemed natural that she should direct where to put the White Elephant stall, whether to have jigsaws with Books or with Toys, and what sort of clothes should go on the Nearly New rail. No wonder everyone assumed she was the club manager's wife! And why not? She was well dressed, nicely spoken and accompanied by her badge of respectability: her friendly and pleasant eleven-year-old daughter. They both worked diligently, falling on each new bagful as it arrived and spreading the contents on the trestles with twice the vigour of anyone else, accompanying their actions with jokes and hummed snatches of tunes. It was a merry, all-girls-together atmosphere – for as soon as the trestles had been erected and the heaviest boxes and bags brought in the men began to melt away.

Through it all the innocent, genuine helpers remained totally unaware that their operation was being systematically looted. All were so absorbed in the process of sorting that they neither saw the filling of the carefully hidden and camouflaged black plastic sacks, nor thought to wonder why the woman and her daughter made so many trips to that particular corner of the room. By the time the pace slackened and everyone else began looking around, Mrs and Miss X were well contented with their haul and set to make their getaway – which they might have achieved had not the club manager felt guilty at his overlong attendance at the bar, and returned to lend a hand.

Just as he approached the room where the jumble was now spread out, the thieves were dragging their bulging bags from the corner, and with supreme confidence – not a nervous twitch or stutter between them – were issuing gay goodbyes to all their 'friends'. Obviously the bags, which were almost as tall as the daughter and twice as round, could not pass totally unexplained, but in that carefully contrived atmosphere of *bonhomie* a few glib words from the mother's practised tongue were enough to satisfy the helpers. No, she explained, they couldn't stay for a cup of tea, much as they'd love to, but they'd got guests coming for the weekend and, what with having to help at the sale the next day, there was *so* much to do that evening. Nobody minded if they took a few things, did they? Nothing much, just bits – they'd pay in the morning.

And with that they would have sailed off into the night, never to be seen again . . . had they not come up against the club manager as he reached the doorway. Whether he rumbled them with a flash of insight or had a naturally disapproving expression that threw the woman off balance, or whether she became over-confident and went too far, no one will ever know. Instead of wisely standing back to let him pass and then silently leaving, she button-holed him with a bright smile; *so* glad he'd arrived, she gushed, they would pay him for their odds and ends now rather than wait until morning. There wasn't much, just a few dresses for her little girl and some blankets for the dogs' beds (the daughter demonstrated the truth of this by plucking at the rough woven material that over-topped the contents of both bags). Then the woman offered two fifty-pence pieces – one for each bag – with the air of one bestowing a generous tip, and knowing it to be so.

But the club manager had advantages over the other helpers; he had not been lulled into a false feeling of friendship towards the couple, and he was the only one who didn't take them for his wife and daughter (although this fact was just now dawning on those nearest the scene). He was certainly not prepared to accept just £1 from these strangers in exchange for what was obviously more than 'a few dresses and blankets' and insisted that the sacks be emptied and each item priced. And those items were many and varied: each and every good piece from the White Elephant stall was found carefully wrapped in the most perfect of the clothes, which ranged from vests to fit a new-born infant to an overcoat for a twenty-stone gentleman. The fact that they had been discovered seemed to give the couple no discomfort at all; they stood by in total indifference as the goodies were revealed, and when accusing eyes were turned towards them the woman shrugged her shoulders and said mildly that some you win, some you lose and would they take a fiver for the lot instead?

After the pair had been sent off empty-handed and the duped helpers were able thoroughly to enjoy delicious outrage and a good gossip they realised just how clever the woman had been, first in knowing or guessing when the layout was to be, then in allowing everyone to think she

75

was firmly connected with the club – without ever actually saying so. She had very quickly struck up acquaintance with the first helper she met, then used that person's name familiarly to the second and so on until each person had imagined her to be well known to all but themselves. To complete the tale: she and her daughter were later seen selling good second-hand clothes in a nearby market, acquired no doubt from jumble sale layouts where nothing had occurred to unmask their duplicity.

But, you may think, characters with such bare-faced cheek must be few and far between, and anyway you and your friends would never fall for a trick like that! As, no doubt, the Ladies' Group in a Somerset town also confidently believed . . . until recently.

The boy who came to help at their jumble sale was about sixteen years old, with wholesome good looks and frank, ingenuous blue eyes that easily danced with laughter, especially when he teased and flattered the ladies of the group, never taking his jokes too far and always remaining good-natured and biddable. He soon latched onto the White Elephant stall and positioned himself between the two lady members directed to run it, where he kept them pink with pleasure and wreathed in smiles until the hall doors were flung open, then turned the force of his charm towards the customers. He sold items worth ten pence for fifty and those worth fifty for £1; he made one woman feel that life had never been complete without a wok, while another really needed an umbrella when all she'd come in for was a bikini and some sunglasses. He sent every customer away from the stall with a purchase that would later probably raise the thought 'I wonder what made me buy *that*?' and a bigger hole in the purse than anticipated – yet with a remembered laugh that took the sting out of being 'done'.

When the crowd moved on to the clothing and only one or two customers were left picking over the remains of the White Elephant stall the boy delicately excused himself. After a considerable while one woman helper said to the other, 'Your son's a long time in the toilet.' The second woman gave her a puzzled look. 'He's not *my* son – I thought he was yours!' As the truth dawned, they turned with one accord to gaze into the margarine tub that served as a cash box, to find that every £1 and fifty-pence coin had gone – at least £10, they later estimated, not to mention any that had been slipped unnoticed into the boy's pocket during the selling period. Needless to say, he was never seen again and it's not hard to imagine the brilliant career ahead of a young teenage con-man who has the wit to see the possibilities in a jumble sale and the nerve to carry off such a coup single-handed, with such obvious job satisfaction.

So, how do you guard against this kind of audacity? You could be like the jumble sale organiser for a Royal British Legion branch who, having once been similarly visited by swindlers, now allows no one but members to help and insists that they wear their badges; but she is lucky in having plenty of staff available within the organisation, all proud to wear the emblem.

If you don't feel able to force badges onto your working party for fear they will think you paranoid, you must make it your job to be aware of every unknown face that enters the hall during the layout. Don't assume, because a stranger comes in earnestly chatting to a bona fide member, that they are 'together'; a clever thief can recognise a helper in the street outside and within two minutes can give every impression of being an old friend. It is possible to ask the member to introduce you to the other person without seeming officious, and no harm is done if he or she turns out to be a bosom buddy who has kindly offered to do the club a favour. And, of course, a complete stranger may want to help, without thievery in mind and from a genuine desire to support the fund; or from loneliness, or the forgivable lesser impertinence of wanting first pick of the jumble. It would be a shame to turn away willing hands, so be welcoming, be interested . . . but be watchful. If the newcomer is an honest person, he or she should find such attention flattering, and if not, so restricting that he or she may quickly fade from the scene.

As the organiser with ultimate responsibility for everything, it will pay you not to get too involved with the actual, physical laying out and selling of stock, but rather to stand back and keep an overview of the whole proceedings. During the sale a close watch kept from the customers' side of the trestle can often catch the odd sly slipping of a handful of goods into a bag out of sight of the seller, and a mild 'Excuse me, I think you have forgotten to pay for those' whispered into an ear may elicit a blush, an apology and frantic fumbling in purse or pocket to stump up the necessary. Alternatively, it could produce an emphatic denial which you would be wise to cut short with a sweet smile and a brief (if unmeant) apology – 'If you say you've paid for those things, then I must have been mistaken' – even if you are absolutely certain that you are right: it is almost impossible to prove that the customer *didn't* give the money to a helper further along the table. Dignified backing down will only lose the fund a few pennies, while it's unlikely the thief will try any more pilfering that day.

Probably the most sickening of all is the mother who has taught her tiny child to steal – often tins from the Produce stall that the babe drops, to order, into Mummy's open and carefully unattended bag. If you confront the woman she will deny any knowledge and heap hair-raising curses on the bewildered child, often slapping it hard to stop it revealing that it was she who told it what to take. All you can do is gently relieve the child of its booty before it gets back to Mum and warn it that you are watching its every move. Whether you report the mother to the authorities is up to you.

Very often customers will prefer to gather an armful of clothing as they browse along the row of trestles, paying for the lot when the armful gets too cumbersome. This can be a perfectly legitimate practice, not the least of the benefits being that the fewer times a punter's purse has to be pulled from its safe place, opened and returned, the less mischief can befall it. But, not unnaturally, these customers sometimes arouse deep suspicion, especially among helpers who have already experienced cheats who claim to have paid elsewhere in the hall for goods when it

is quite certain they have not, or have simply walked out of the door with a bundle for which they have not paid tucked 'absent-mindedly' under one arm. The nervousness and suspicion that such a situation can generate will hang like a pall over the stalls, affecting not only the person being watched but all the other jumblers too, and the atmosphere is made worse if the helpers react either with whispering behind hands and heavily accusing looks, or with aggressive demands on the customer that each article is paid for as it is selected.

There is, in fact, a far happier way of dealing with the problem and you should brief your staff on it before the sale starts. The helper who first notices the growing armful of clothes should suggest that the unwieldy collection is handed to him or her to be 'put by' behind the stall, then any more items the customer chooses can be sent back along the line to be added to the pile and payment can be made in one lot at the customer's convenience. The invitation can be given quite pleasantly and is of such obvious advantage to the honest shopper that anyone who turns it down deserves to be kept under surveillance for the rest of the sale!

Now to another cheeky criminal: the one who claims and takes away other people's bags of shopping that have been put behind a stall. A jumble-bug acquaintance of mine makes a habit of asking the helpers on the White Elephant stall to look after his first gleanings (generally heavy, bulky and breakable) while he goes back over their trestle for any little gems he might have missed. Imagine his shocked disbelief at one sale when he realised the youth standing next to him was pointing to the very pile he had so recently fought and paid for and entrusted to the helper's care. What's more, the spotty oik was confidently claiming, 'Yeah, that's the stuff. Me mate arst me to pick it up fer 'im.' Of course, my friend indignantly challenged the youth's claim and was able, fortunately, to convince the poor helper, who finally owned to a dim recollection of selling those items to him; though truth to tell her memory of the customers she had served in the Great Rush was but a blur. The boy, cheerfully unabashed, decided to cut his losses and ducked out with the comment that he must have been told to collect the wrong stuff and "e'd find 'is mate'. . . .

The only reason his little ruse failed was that, busy watching what was bought and what happened to it, he failed to take note of the buyer. And literally 'taking note' of the buyer is exactly the way your helpers can combat this rogue. It takes no more than ten seconds to jot down the sex and a distinguishing feature of a customer on a slip of paper and include it with their purchases, out of sight of scheming eyes. When someone claims the shopping, a swift glance at the written note should satisfy that it is going to the right owner; and if someone claims it for a friend they must be asked to describe him or her. If they can't, or their description doesn't tally (and remember, if the helpers have had to look hard at the customer to write the note in the first place there is more chance of them remembering other features), then the purchaser must be required to appear in person. It's better to have one slightly irritated customer than an outraged one whose triumphantly won booty has been carelessly given away. The only snag with this method is when a witty yet careless helper notes down the more comical or unfortunate features of the customer then forgetfully leaves the description amongst his or her goods!

A variation on the theme is for the customers to write their own names on the slips – but beware, a name spoken out loud for the *helper* to write down is playing right into the thief's hands, for all he or she has to do is approach another helper and say: 'Mr King (or Smith, Jones, etc.) asked me to collect his bag – it's that one on the end' or 'Can I have my bag please – I'm Mr King'. With his knowledge of both the bag and the rightful owner's name, who will doubt his authority?

Other solutions to the problem may come to mind, but the easiest – refusing to look after shoppers' bags – is not to be recommended, being unkind and unproductive. Turning over clothes is tiring enough without the weight of various carrier-bags hampering one's progress; and an overladen shopper slows down the flow of movement along the trestles, takes up twice the room and gets in everyone's way.

At the tag-end of this catalogue of thieves and rogues are those who steal from the person. These are occasionally professional pickpockets who have realised that jumble sale customers just might be wearing expensive jewellery or have cheque books and credit cards in their pockets, but they are most frequently just opportunist criminals who spot a carelessly dropped purse and are swift to adopt it as their own. You can but fume impotently at the stupidity of the general public who seem set on making life as easy as possible for the thief; for instance, all those little old ladies, nervous of leaving their valuables at home, who bring wheeled shopping bags ('trolleys') laden with bank, pension and post office books, cash and the family heirlooms – then abandon them in the corner of the room with the fond idea that one of your overworked helpers will keep an eye on them!

With a bit of luck your warning at the end of the second committee meeting will have been passed on to (and taken to heart by) most of the helpers, so they will arrive with very few valuables about them, but it is always wise to have a really safe place to put things belonging to those who didn't get, or heed, the message – perhaps along with the old ladies' trolleys. Very often the kitchen is the only place, though it is not foolproof or particularly hygienic.

One hall in a Dorset market town had a very convenient area for piling coats and bags, just behind the kitchen door – which was usually kept open – until a sharp-eyed opportunist spotted the possibilities and blighted half a dozen sales before a warning notice could be pinned up. Because of the shape of the kitchen, for most of the time the staff had their backs to the door and the dim little corner behind it, and if ever they glimpsed the rear end of a figure bent over the heap of possessions they had no reason to believe it to be anyone other than a helper searching for her purse or a handkerchief. Meanwhile, customers buying tea at the hatch might clearly have seen the door and the up-ended figure behind it, but not recognised the swift search being made of all the pockets and bags – or even suspected that someone was up to no good. It has always been assumed that the thief was a woman, mainly because most of the helpers at the six sales so afflicted were women, but she was never caught.

The first rule, therefore, is to keep the kitchen door shut at all times, the second to have the collection of personal possessions in a place clearly visible to the helpers but out of sight of customers (and thieves): a cupboard under the work-top, for instance. If the business of removing a purse from a handbag so carefully stored gets in the way of the tea ladies, then it is unlikely to be attempted by anyone but the genuine owner.

This gloomy list of evil-doers may make you wonder if

all your customers are likely to be criminals, especially when you learn that I was witness to all but one of these examples (that one was told me by the victim himself). However, these events *were* spread over my twenty-five-year experience of ardent jumblophilia, so you would have to be very unlucky indeed to catch even one rogue at work at your sale. And, as forewarned is forearmed, you will probably find that, without temptation put in their way, your helpers and customers will be as good as gold.

The last word has to be about dealers – not to confer on them criminal tendencies but to acknowledge their smooth tongues and bare-faced cheek. One or more may very well knock on the door and offer plausible, even moving reasons for being allowed a pre-sale pick of the goodies; to which end they will glibly offer to pay more than regular customers for any items they select, or an enhanced entry fee of fifty pence or £1. However, you are unlikely to make much profit from them in the long run, as they are skilled at bargaining and pointing out the odd flaw in an item to make you drop your price. Above all, the helpers and jumblers alike will be *most* resentful of any privilege allowed to dealers, who are all well known to the true jumble-bug and generally considered to be the most predatory of all punters. If you listen to a group of jumblers talking shop you will often hear the comment 'I wouldn't go to that jumble sale, they let the dealers in early', clearly a warning not to be taken lightly. And do bear in mind that dealers rarely stay to spend on Refreshments or the Raffle, many of them not even bothering to glance at the Clothing stalls. Unless you positively relish a verbal tussle and can be sure of making an exceedingly good profit from a dealer, it's really not worth the risk of upsetting your helpers and customers by showing anybody preferential treatment.

# CHAPTER TEN

## This is IT!

The hands of the hall clock are moving ever closer to opening time. You have checked the stalls and made sure that no one will be able to sell the helpers' coats or any of the hall property (don't laugh, that really can happen: a helper was once tickled pink to have sold 'that old boiler thing' for £2 – that is, until he was told it was the tea-urn and would cost over £40 to replace).

You have advised the helpers on what to do if they are suspicious of any customer, and told them why you will be roving round the hall rather than standing behind a trestle, so if they need help of any kind they have only to catch your eye. Please make sure they all realise that buying at jumble sales is strictly a 'hands-on' business; if a customer at one end of the trestle asks how much is, say, that lampshade at the other end, the helper should not begin to answer until she has picked up the item and placed it in the customer's hand – otherwise someone standing next to the lampshade will prick up his or her ears and think 'Only fifty pence? I'll have that', and by the time the first customer has agreed to buy, the other has a firm hold of the bargain and is proffering the stated amount. Possession is certainly ten-tenths of the law at a jumble sale, and it matters not how much the dispossessed customer may complain – the spoils go to those with the long arm and firm grasp!

Occasionally two hands may descend on one object at the same time and an unseemly tugging match ensues, with heightening temper on both sides; or two people may simultaneously pick up the separate pieces of a pair, be it ornaments or clothes, and neither will give up their share. This is your cue for an auction. First remove the disputed item or items from the customers' clutches then suggest a starting price. If one agrees to that, look to the other and ask if they would like to offer more, and so on until one drops out.

This was once put into practice in a pretty village in the Quantocks, where two red-faced matrons were coming to blows over a glass pig. The helper, who couldn't imagine why it was worth fighting over, was becoming quite distraught until an interested spectator, who had recognised the ornament as a rare Bristol blue glass piece and knew why the ladies were both so determined, suggested an auction and kindly took over as auctioneer. The helper was astounded when the price began at the fifty pence she had originally rather diffidently suggested (fully expecting to come down later) and rose in tenpenny hops, finally to stick at £6.20. As for the lady customers, both triumph and disappointment were evenly tempered, for the winner's profit margin had been whittled down more than she liked whilst the loser was smugly aware of that fact – and everyone else in the hall had thoroughly enjoyed the little drama.

## What to Charge

It is often assumed that anyone can stand behind a trestle and sell, but when it comes to putting a price on items many people find they are simply at a loss. On one hand they want to do as well for the fund as possible, but on the other, with a flesh-and-blood customer standing in front of them, they lose their nerve and stammer out a ludicrously low sum, even when they know they should be asking more. And if, in pre-sale panic, they seek advice from their colleagues on either side they are likely to find one a dragon, firmly resolved to demand high prices, and the other a mouse who thinks that asking more than five pence is an awful cheek.

You might go along with the opinions of your helpers and feel that the disparity is not worth bothering about: with such a pattern of high and low asking prices, in theory one should balance the other, resulting in a reasonable average profit; but it is easily forgotten that, while customers may seem totally engrossed in sorting through the goods you have on offer, their ears are still working (and most acutely!). If they hear one helper asking far higher prices than another it doesn't take genius to work out which one will get their custom.

As you can't change the various temperaments of your staff – or label every item to remove the element of chance – you must settle for the best solution available; and that lies in encouraging the helpers to discuss, before the sale, the sort of prices they intend to charge. Less experienced members or those lacking confidence may be surprised to learn of the sums others feel they can reasonably ask and may be happy to bring themselves into line with the majority, whilst the more aggressive 'squeeze 'em till the pips squeak' individuals, once identified, can at least be asked to moderate their demands (though they seldom do).

Incidentally, if staff are unsure when asked 'how much?' they might pause to consider, then tentatively suggest a sum as if inviting negotiation – a chance to bargain that, as often as not, will be taken up by the customer with some alacrity; but a price given instantly in a firm 'take it or leave it' voice is usually accepted without question.

Having once encouraged most of your helpers to think along the same lines for general pricing, you can then introduce those on the jumble stalls to the idea that, during the initial fevered excitement of the Great Rush, nothing should be sold for less than twenty pence, except, perhaps, small toys and negligible items of clothing. If the customer is not prepared to pay the suggested price, the helper shouldn't haggle at this stage, because the next person along may think the item a wonderful buy and be happy to give the full amount. Only when the press of bodies begins to thin out and items are picked up with less frenzy and more thoughtfulness should bargaining and price-dropping be considered; and when there are more people preparing to leave than there are still shopping it will be time to announce 'fifty pence a carrier-bagful' or 'an armful'.

## Opening Time

But for now you have the sale still ahead of you. With luck, your staff will have taken your briefings in good part and all should be raring to go – or eager to get it over with. Calm them down with a free cup of tea or coffee while the crowd outside are being soothed by their warming beverages, the pennies paid for which are making a good start to your fundraising effort. Now you can anticipate opening the doors, which is best done *exactly two minutes before time*. Oh, how petty, you may think. But imagine if you'd been standing on the same spot for anything up to an hour, probably in a draught, possibly in rain, snow or a howling gale, looking at your watch only to find the hands had hardly moved, willing time to go faster; just think how grateful you would be not to have to stand there for those last, unbearable two minutes – for any of those one hundred and twenty snail's-pace seconds! However, there's a fine balance between easing the lot of those who come early and incurring the righteous indignation of those who arrive dead on time, only to find the sale half over.

But, oh, having said that, the delicious lingering memory of the sale that opened a whole hour early because the helpers didn't like to think of the customers standing outside in what was a veritable deluge! It was a sale of so many bargains that, three hours later, this customer was still plumbing unsorted depths and coming up triumphant, so for once the ultra-early opening didn't matter at all.

Opening late always matters and should never be indulged in; if you're not ready on time, better to open the doors and let the hordes in to do your sorting for you than keep them snorting and pawing at the ground outside for a minute longer than advertised. And when you do open, be sure to charge a ten pence admission fee: it's not just acceptable, it is expected, and you gain no gratitude by waiving it, neither will free admission cause more people to attend your sale than otherwise. Why miss out on the easiest source of revenue? An idle count of one Saturday afternoon queue for a sale in a village two miles outside a small county town came to more than one hundred persons – an instant profit of over £10 on the door alone! On a practical level, a sign stating the admission fee should be put up in a position clearly visible to everyone joining the queue so they can have the correct sum ready to hand over.

## The Left-overs

Under your informed and far-sighted management the sale should be smooth-running, handsomely repaying all the hard work involved; but towards the end you will all begin to be aware of quite how hard that work has been. Just when you think the pace is slowing and, maybe, you can relax, there are decisions to be made; although you will probably have no difficulty judging when the time is ripe to reduce the price of the jumble, the good-quality items on the Prestige stalls will need some thought. Do you sell them cheaply on the 'everything must go' principle, or is it reasonable to store them for some money-making event in the future? Often, it's a case of putting by some, and almost giving away others which, whilst being perfectly good items, don't seem to appeal to your customers and have been doing the rounds of sales and coffee mornings for as long as you can remember.

Tired and inwardly groaning as your helpers may be at the thought of repacking the left-overs, it will be worth making an effort to change their attitude towards this job. No one likes to see good items going to the rubbish tip, and it only takes a little imagination to find a splendid new life for some of them. For instance, a satin or lurex dress that may have been over-the-top for your customers could, with a little adjustment, dress an angel for the school nativity play or a fairy for the local amateur dramatics club pantomime. Perhaps Hallowe'en night is looming so a sack full of black garments to be turned into witches' and warlocks' costumes might be welcome at a children's club, whilst earlier in the year bright and shiny fabrics might be used by all sorts of groups involved in the local carnival.

There may be among your number those involved with child-minding, the nursery school, a playgroup, holiday play schemes or clubs for slightly older children. If nudged into thought these people may find a wealth of useful items left over on your trestles. Beginning with the most prosaic, always useful are absorbent cotton rags for mop-ping up, aprons and overalls of all sizes and small nether-garments in case of accidents, whilst of play value are patty tins and safe kitchen tools for fun in the sandpit, sieves and plastic containers for water-play and exciting additions to that good old standby – the dressing-up box. And don't forget that the tiniest baby clothes might fit dollies and teddies.

A cotton sheet is larger and more durable than the biggest sheet of art paper. Marked with checks and tautly pegged out on the grass it can provide a giant draughts and chess board (children can improvise their own pieces, such as chessmen from appropriately decorated large and medium plastic fizzy drinks bottles, weighted with sand or water) or it can be painted in the form of other board games. Likewise pegged out it can be a canvas for a hilarious body-painting session resulting in a bright, abstract mural, or for a more careful and absorbing exercise it can be painted as a map of the area. Blankets and sheets can quickly be converted into tents by draping them over a low line or by wrapping two or three round a tripod of sticks for a Red Indian wigwam.

Plain cotton garments, especially T-shirts, can be fun to decorate with fabric paints, whilst older children might like to try tie-dyeing or the Indonesian craft of batik.

Some of your ladies may be involved with the sewing bees that provide beautiful items for the fête's craftwork stall, and they will certainly have their eyes open for any really good material, or woollens that can be unravelled for re-knitting as something else; but has anyone ever considered furnishing an old-fashioned pedlar's tray with haberdashery items culled from jumble sales. Especially charming at a period street fair, where all the workers wear costume, is a simple tray hung from a cord round the neck and strewn with cards of pretty buttons, buckles, shoe-laces and trimmings, lengths of lace and lace inserts, ribbons and cords of all sorts, braids and fringings, bunches of fabric flowers, beads and brooches, hatpins, knobpins, knitting pins, safety pins and pincushions; many of these items can be hung from the sides and front of the tray or pinned to the seller's bodice. And once your helpers are primed to look out for such tools and trimmings the clearing-up process becomes far more interesting, with everyone proudly showing off their well-spotted finds.

Still with the fête in mind, perhaps someone would like to take charge of all the china left-overs from the White Elephant stall and use them as a basis for a china-smashing booth (three balls for ten pence – and who can resist such satisfying misbehaviour?).

If you have arranged for dealers to collect the residue, yet plan on stripping every useful item from the collection, do make sure that the process has finished and everything is boxed and bagged before they arrive; part of their reward for taking on your rubbish disposal is to have cotton waste to sell for pulping, and decent garments for resale in the market, so they won't be happy watching you pinching their profits!

And that's it – the sale's over, the hall looks as if you've never been there and you're exhausted yet elated. It was fun and worthwhile, you have some hilarious stories to tell of peculiar customers, and a few marvellous bargains that will amaze everyone . . . 'But, my dear, why on earth should anyone throw that away? It's simply gorgeous!' You think there's something to be said for this jumble sale lark, after all? Read on.

## PART TWO: IN FRONT OF THE TRESTLE

# CHAPTER ELEVEN

## *How to Incubate a Jumble-bug*

If you suggest to anyone that they sort through a roomful of miscellaneous junk that once belonged to a lot of strangers there will nearly always be a definite reaction: either their eyes light up with excitement or they shudder in distaste. Rarely do they give a Gallic shrug and suggest they just come along for the ride. So, on the ground that the only contact jumble *haters* would have with a book like this is gingerly between finger and thumb as they transfer it to the rubbish bin, it can be assumed that any reader committed to studying this and the following chapters must have the makings of a jumbler . . . or be a mole for the organisers! (Get your own back, jumble-bugs – read Part One.)

In which case, you probably already have a strong streak of common sense, a deal of optimism, patience, curiosity and a certain amount of avarice; you will also need strong arms, good feet and a thick skin. Rid yourself of squeamishness and embarrassment; it has been a long time since the trestle was the sole province of the poor, the dirty or the diseased; your practical mind and the evidence of your own eyes should convince you that the goodies you choose to bring home are first-class, and that once most items of clothing are laundered they bear little or no trace of the original wearers. And think of antiques, where the patina of much handling by previous owners is not just accepted but prized.

As for the disdain of neighbours, can you be sure it isn't jealousy? Once you have established that jumbling is your hobby (your enthusiasm and love of showing off eccentric tenpenny purchases will do this) they may even let slip that they admire your prowess in the field, and the only reason they don't go jumbling themselves is that they don't seem to find the bargains as you do.

Their problem is lack of method.

Most of them attend the first jumble sale that attracts their attention, arrive only a few minutes before it's due to start so surge in behind the majority and soon fall victim to the frustration of not being able to penetrate the wall of bodies that quickly obscures every stall. They are reduced to tugging at likely pieces of material glimpsed briefly between the busy, shifting forms, and rarely drag out anything suitable for their own purposes. This situation breeds defeatism and dissatisfaction so, when the next jumble sale advertisements are posted, though their hearts may quicken at the thought of the bargains that could be waiting they are quickly sobered by their previous lack of success.

## Begin at the Beginning – Choose the Right Jumble Sale

The best jumble sale is one where you are a helper. Even if it does mean a lot of work, having first pick of the boxes and bags you get to sort through is worth all the energy expended; and a few hours spent as a helper can be more rewarding than being first in the queue at three other jumble sales. However, other people have a sound grasp of this principle and are not so likely to relinquish such perks to a stranger; you have to be well connected with a society or organisation before being allowed to run barefoot through its bric-à-brac.

So you have mostly to be a customer; and if you are a tyro you may think the cosy, painless way to start is at a little local affair. But this is not necessarily so, especially if you are female and aware of your 'image'. At a local sale there will be people – helpers and other shoppers – with whom you already have passing acquaintance and you could become far too self-conscious to buy anything under their eagle eyes. Even if you find a stretch of tables blessedly free of familiar faces, the goods themselves will make you doubtful; that may be a lovely dress, but did it once belong to a neighbour who will recognise it? Or even worse, to someone so notorious that the whole neighbourhood will recognise it and tar you with the same brush! Even if you have a blithe disregard for what the gossipers might say, you can still find yourself at a disadvantage. It is very easy for a helper to ask a higher price of someone he or she knows and very difficult for a shopper to haggle with an acquaintance, however slight, so the bags of jumble you take home will be rather less than the bargains you hoped for and your feelings about jumble sales less happy because you were forced to pay more than you wanted to.

Much better to go to another district, where you can elbow ribs and stamp on toes with much the same vigorous unconcern as the others apply to yours; where you can join the unseemly dash and grab with enthusiasm and even a little greed; where you can pile up an armful of the oddest purchases without worrying about appearances, and haggle without feeling quite so mean. And you can come home with a bag full of items never before seen in your locality.

Should you choose to begin your jumbling career between late May and early September, finding a jumble sale to go to amongst the other summer activities can be a little difficult as these holiday months are 'out of season'; however, a few are to be found here and there and one on a sunny afternoon can be a pleasant introduction to the pastime. To begin with, the queue is likely to be smaller (without the dealers and car booters who will be frantically dashing from fête to fête) and at the front will be the hard-core jumblers, people for whom a weekend without a jumble sale is as tasteless as a hard-boiled egg without salt and pepper. For these addicts even the poorest sort of sale is better than no jumble at all, and they will travel a long way to attend the only one advertised in the local paper. They are worth cultivating. From them you can gain much local knowledge: which sales are over-priced; which are run by gorgons who create a patronising or suspicious atmosphere; which seem to have the best-quality clothing or excellent and abundant bric-à-brac. They will be full of hilarious stories of sales long gone and will be able to tell you exactly where they bought each item they are wearing – every piece of it jumble, of course – and how much it cost; and they might even tell you of a good sale coming up that you would otherwise not know about. These people rarely give away anything about their private lives and tend to accept newcomers at face value. You may find you make a whole new set of friends amongst whom you can be a totally different person, whilst their company will help to take the boredom out of queuing.

Once you have experienced the exhilaration of the Great Rush and savoured the taste of a good bargain or two, your approach to reading the local paper will be deeply affected. Even if you do manage to restrain your urge to turn directly to the 'What's On' page where the jumble sales are advertised you will only be prolonging the suspense – just as, when you were a child, you picked all the cherries out of your serving of fruit salad and kept them at the side of your dish to enjoy last of all.

And there will come a time when you will feel you are being offered every cherry in the bowl; such agony that you can't eat them all! During the year there are two high seasons for jumble sales: from mid-January until Easter and from the start of the school year in September until just before Christmas. At the heart of either of those periods the large number of advertisements at any one time will send your spirits soaring – then plummeting as you realise the concentration needed just to decide which few you can attend. It is worth having a good selection of felt-tipped pens, a local map, a pocket notebook and a diary or calendar by you when you begin quartering this page.

Begin by marking all the jumble sales to distinguish them from other events, and check that the volume of entries hasn't been so great that other jumble ads have been craftily slipped into another column on another page – newspaper editors in general not being aware of the tragedy of a missed sale. Second, look at the date on each marked entry. Most will be for the same day (Saturday or market day), a few might be for evenings during the week and one or two might fool you by being for the following week; the most experienced jumblers have been known to turn up on the wrong day from careless reading of the ad. How do I know? Ah, well . . . someone must have told me. Note down on your calendar or in your diary any of these advance notices because, whatever you think, you won't remember during the week to look at the paper again, and anyway, you need to cross out any advertisements that are not for the main jumble sale day. What you have left will be difficult enough to arrange, without complicating the issue further.

Now it might be possible to delete a few jumble sales that are too far away – more if you are reliant on public transport or walking. In this case you might be left with just those in the centre of town as possibilities and, restricted as you are by the number of full bags you can heave from place to place, of those remaining few sales you will want to choose two or three that promise to be most rewarding. A large or heavy bargain may be worth the hire of a taxi to get home, but half a dozen bags of mixed clothing, picked up at various mediocre sales, might, under closer scrutiny, prove to have been unworthy of the fare.

Car owners must temper enthusiasm with a regard for the cost of petrol and parking and the time wasted in driving from car park to car park (and round and round . . .). If you can't resist visiting as many sales as possible, choose the ones in the centre of town and plan to park centrally, going back to your car after each sale to stow your bags and then walking to the next one. Knowledge of how to get from hall to hall in the shortest time and by the shortest route through crowded streets can become a source of great pride – especially your cunning use of buildings and car parks with convenient back exits that aren't marked on the map. Your street map is important and will soon become a treasured document. It is worth marking all the schools, churches and halls in bright marker pen to make them quicker to find in a hurry (and you'll always be in a hurry when flitting to the next sale).

With the easy part over, the remaining advertisements must now be judged on timing versus possible content. Annoyingly, the sales that fit neatly one after the other, all nicely grouped in one area, might appear far less interesting than a lone renegade that completely upsets the timetable. But what is it that makes a certain jumble sale look more promising than another, especially when the advertising formats of both are almost identical?

Well, the answer lies less in boasts of 'Grand', 'Huge' or 'Bumper' than in the name at the top of the advertisement – the group or charity running the sale; and then it depends on what you want to buy. A jumble run by a nursery, playgroup or infant school will have a high proportion of maternity wear, baby and toddler clothes, children's books and toys – wonderful if you are just launching into parenthood yourself – but the chances of finding antiques on its White Elephant stall or designer labels amongst the clothes are low. A sale involving enthusiastic youngsters, of an age to collect door to door, will probably have a great deal of stock ranging from good quality down to absolute rubbish as the children will be totally impartial in whom they ask for jumble. Children see no reason why anyone should be left out of their fundraising drive, expect to be given something at every door, and generally are, because they are not easy to turn away. Clubs with a high proportion of independent elderly members may throw up some gems of early-twentieth-century collectables as well as classic clothes and the odd stoutly boned corset, but state-run old people's homes tend to be less rewarding. They rely on generosity from the surrounding dwellings as the inmates have very little left to give; and have also an added difficulty collecting stock, everybody involved being either too infirm or too busy.

Class, although it may not be the done thing to say so, has great bearing on what you are likely to find on the trestle, so a council estate sale will be full of children's clothes and cheap and cheerful, once fashionable clothing-catalogue stuff; a village sale will be representative of all

the people who occupy its various buildings so its stock will be most mixed, whilst a superior club of predominantly mature, genteel ladies will yield garments in muted tones with Jaeger and Edinburgh Wool Shop labels, a great deal of Marks & Spencer's old stock and rather nice toiletries. The latter group's prices may be ultra-high (they have a militant organiser) or negligible (they can't understand why anyone should pay *anything* for their cast-offs).

There are, of course, many exceptions to the rule. It may seem logical that a Labour Party sale in a staunch Tory stronghold would not attract stock of any great amount or interest, but if the organiser is fired with a need to show the opposition just what his or her small band can do, and can whip the supporters into enthusiastic collecting, it might be the best sale around. This is where local knowledge gives the edge; if Bill Bloggs made a good job of it last year, there's a chance that he'll be expected to do even better this time – and someone around will know if he's going to try!

But no one has ever found the perfect method for getting to know in advance how good or bad a sale in another district will be, and serendipity often beats logic. By rights a particular group should have very little on its tables because the club has few members and is in an isolated community where there have been a lot of other sales recently; however, Mrs Jones's son from Bristol is emigrating and, at her request, brought a car full of jumble on his last visit, poor Mr Edward's mother died in Paignton and he hates the thought that her worthless little treasures should be thrown away by heartless house-clearance men, so has brought them home and doesn't know what to do with them, and Mr Biggs up at the big house has just brought home a new wife, as eager to make her mark in the village as she is to obliterate every trace of her predecessor. Even the organiser and helpers have no way of knowing what a stupendous sale theirs is likely to be until all the bags and boxes begin arriving, so how can potential customers do so?

Sadly, it can work the other way: many small, disparate coincidences of time and place can make an eagerly awaited event that last year was a triumph into a disappointing flop; but a true jumble-bug puts it down to experience and looks forward to next week's sales with a fervour heightened by frustration. Yet again, that flop may be someone else's greatest victory, if they spot and grab one uncharacteristically good piece amongst the junk.

There is some truth in the view that the less familiar the helpers are with minor antiques, collectables or good-quality clothing the less likely they are to recognise and claim them for themselves (or, to be fair, take them to a dealer for the good of the fund). My favourite shirt is made of heavy, dull raw silk that drapes beautifully and, if rolled into a ball in the hand, bursts open again like a living thing, an opening flower bud, to show not a crease. Most unexpectedly I came across it at a very down-market sale (but the only one advertised that weekend) where the helpers thought all silk was thin and shiny and that this particular garment was damaged anyway, although those dark flecks might wash out, if I was lucky; how much more fun I had buying that shirt for ten pence than I would have had in a shop with the assistant pointing out all its good points and telling me £50 was really very little to pay for such quality.

Some jumble-bugs will tear round to as many sales as possible, without bothering to consider beforehand whether they are likely to contain good jumble or not; but to get the best of whatever is on offer they aim always to be somewhere near the front of the queue, and are likely to arrive an hour early for the first sale of the day. They know from experience that, by the time they have inspected that particular load of jumble, they will be too late to secure a decent place in the queue for any sale that begins half an hour later, but could be well positioned for one starting on the hour. However, they also find that, if time allows, a very short detour to spend a few minutes casting a glance over what remains of a sale which is almost over can be rewarding; with all the other eagle-eyes already en route for whichever sales they have decided to attend next, a fresh look at trestles already feverishly scoured might find something worthwhile that has been overlooked in haste.

To be as flexible as possible you need to write in a notebook all the sales in chronological order and spend time poring over your map to work out how to get from one to another. Then be sure to take both notebook and map with you; rare is the memory that can recall at will all the details of all the advertisements.

## The Jumbler's Kit

In fact, you might very well give thought to having a certain collection of items that are kept purely for jumbling, just as a doctor will have his bag of drugs for home visits, or a detective the murder bag to take to a suspicious death. Your equipment will need to be carried in something that leaves your arms free for rummaging. This can be a shoulder bag, slung across you like a child's satchel to save having to hitch it up onto your shoulder every few minutes; but after a while the strap may tend to cut into the muscles beside the neck (cure this by making use of the shoulder protector from an old guitar strap or camera case; if you can find one at a jumble sale, of course). Another method is to wear a comfortable garment – trousers, waistcoat or jacket – with voluminous but securely zipped or buttoned pockets; the snag is that such sturdy construction may be a bit too hot in the summer. Best of all is one of those pouch-like 'bum-bags', designed originally to keep skier's valuables safe but then taken up by youngsters as a fashion accessory and now used by slightly older people who can recognise a boon to comfort when they see one. True, it can look a little odd on some figures – but who's worried, at a jumble sale?

Into your bag or pockets will go a purse containing all your loose change, and a folder with a £5 or £10 note in it, to spend only if you are tempted by something out of the run of ordinary jumble and obviously very good – it can happen. With the treasury note include a form of identification and secure the wallet or folder in a separate compartment, for safety's sake. Add to your equipment the notebook and a map, a pen and a number of those very tough, thin plastic carriers given away at supermarkets; they fold up to make a surprisingly small package and you can easily carry enough for four good jumble sales at a time. A few paper tissues are handy because you won't want to abandon your place in the queue to go back to the car if your nose runs, and they are also useful to wrap up small treasures. To be super-efficient you will be sure to carry a tape measure for sizing all those garments that have either lost their labels or, like jeans, look as if they might have shrunk in the wash, and a small pair of scissors to cut beautiful buttons or lace and good zips from tatty material – why bother to take home the whole hideous article if all you want are the trimmings?

For reasons of security, make sure that nothing you carry is worth much, in either real or sentimental value; purses are often put down in the heat of the grab and either stolen or sold, whilst a bag gaping invitingly open may be dipped into. Look out for a plastic wallet or card case and a purse at various jumble sales and keep them solely for jumbling, so that if you lose anything only the contents will matter – a few pounds at worst. And have in a pocket at all times a little money, enough either to use the telephone or to catch a bus home, just in case. And there's also the chance that you might find yourself in the third queue of the day with no small change to pay for your admission, thus committing the worst crime in the jumbling rule book: you will *never* be forgiven if you keep the queue waiting whilst you ask for change, so some five-and tenpence pieces in your pocket can not only save the day but your reputation, too!

Make sure everything you carry is as light-weight as possible – and that goes for weather protection as well. In winter you will probably be standing in pouring rain and a howling gale one minute, then the next under lights in a heated room, tightly latched into a rugby scrum with a dozen other steaming bodies. Dressing for comfort whilst jumbling matters at all times but especially under these conditions, and a loose, thin, but windproof mackintosh that can be whipped off, rolled into a ball and stuffed into your bag as the crowd begins to shuffle in will actually give you an advantage over those in bulkier rain-sodden garb.

Gloves and scarves, unless of dish-rag floppiness, are notorious for wilfully leaping from pockets and should be chosen very carefully; remember, at the time when you strip them off and stuff them away, your mind and eyes will be fixed on the trestles ahead and your hands will be on automatic pilot. Other garments should be light and unrestricting, allowing your arms far more eccentric movements than they are likely to make at all other times (except perhaps at yoga or aerobic classes).

Footwear – and for obvious reasons peep-toe stilettos are no good to you or others at a jumble sale; the weight of even a small lady is transmuted into that of an elephant when passed down through a shaft of that narrowness. Trainers or walking shoes are ideal, unless they let the feet get wet, for there is no misery like that of standing still for three-quarters of an hour, in a cold foyer with the door open, feeling your wet feet turn into immovable blocks of ice. Draughts will painfully attack even dry feet and legs under such conditions, so good warm socks and trousers are recommended.

For the rest: never carry bulky or wickerwork open baskets. They are easy to steal from, dig into other people's ribs or catch in their clothing so much that they can provoke real aggression, and you will find yourself thumped, stamped on and sworn at by even the mildest jumblers. Wear no unnecessary jewellery to lose amongst the jumble; there is no cry so heart-rending as 'I've lost my gold watch', so if you can find an old working watch at a sale, buy it just to wear whilst jumbling. Try to arrange not to carry any other valuables at all, but if you must, keep them as close as possible to you in a body belt or some sort of pouch – even sew a deep pocket into your bloomers!

A lot of older people are afraid to leave pension, post office and bank books at home in case they are burgled in their absence. Instead, they carry them around in hand-bags that they put down whilst inspecting a nice-looking skirt or jumper, then find a thief has walked off not only with what they wanted to protect, but also the keys to the house as well! Neither is it any protection to put them in a shopping trolley which is then left under the eye of a helper; but it's often done, with various sad results, and some absent-minded ladies have been known to get all the way home before remembering their valuables, which by now are languishing in an empty, locked hall or, far worse, are being gleefully pawed over by an opportunist crook.

Such emphasis on security may seem over-cautious, but there is something very hurtful about being stolen from, or losing a cherished item, whilst in the act of trying to get a bargain; and a hobby once tainted can take a long time to regain its attraction. Jumble sales are an obvious draw for greedy people and opportunists, and those who do not heed this fact have only themselves to blame if their careless attitude causes them loss.

# CHAPTER TWELVE

## *How to be Really Good . . .*

So, comfortably dressed, sensibly shod and suitably equipped, clutching your admission fee in readiness, you are standing in the queue. You are probably twenty minutes early and about twelfth in line, which is not a bad place to be.

In front of you will be the true jumble junkies, those so hooked they simply don't care if an hour's wait results in buying only two tatty paperbacks and a chipped photo-frame, or a skirt that turns out to be too small and a sweater with an indelible stain down the front; whatever their disappointment at one particular sale they none the less will be waiting in the next jumble queue for their 'fix' of bargains.

Being the first customer to arrive is rarely of any great advantage: all that waiting time to think of the goodies that, as the one in pole position, you'll be able to snaffle before the others crowd in! It can only lead to disappoint-ment, for in reality your privileged position merely puts you a split second ahead of your fellow jumblers, and as you won't be able to survey the whole length of the stall in that time you will bitterly resent their swift arrival to either side of you – and their equally fast removal of anything worth buying. Furthermore, unless you have the luck inadvertently to head for the section of stall display-ing what to you would be a good bargain, you'll carry away a deep conviction that you were the only person in the whole hall to choose the one area covered with unmitigated junk. It won't necessarily be true, but that's what it will feel like.

With about five minutes to go to opening time there is a noticeable stiffening of the sinews in those about you. The older members seated on chairs shuffle to their feet, well aware of their exact positions in the queue and determined not to be displaced; those with bags and anti-social angular baskets clutch them tighter to their stomachs, ready to use them as battering rams, and everyone checks, yet again, that they have the correct admission fee in their hands. Someone asks what time it is and watches are consulted.

'I make it three minutes to go,' says one.

'Nar – only two,' says London Stan, sure of himself.

Another voice chips in: 'By my watch we've got four minutes to wait.'

Stan, always quick with an answer, replies, 'Never! You wanna take that watch back where you bought it, gel – get'm ta refund yer tenpence.'

Hilda, right at the front and never the shrinking violet, begins hammering on the door. 'Hey, you in there, open up – it's gone time.'

'Shoot the lock off, Hilda!' shouts one wag.

''Aven't got me gun on me – but I could burn the door down wi' me matches, and smoke the buggers out.'

These few minutes of general jollity, similar to those encountered in the trenches before the troops go over the top, will subside to tense grumbling once the queue decides that the doors are late in opening, and there will be no talking at all between people who are now in contention as they vie for position in the Great Rush. The only sound then will be the thunder of feet.

Most of these will turn immediately towards the White Elephant stall, led there not by telepathy or any mechanical locating device but by the sterling reconnaissance put in by those at the head of the queue. If the doors have glass panels or are open, then you can be sure that this jumble elite has evaluated every piece (be it from a distance) and noted its position; if the doors are blank and firmly closed then a detachment of 'scouts' has been sent out to roam the outside and peer through windows then report back on content and placing of the stalls, while their station in the queue is scrupuously kept for them. During their absence, the wily, 'frail' senior members use their age and wisdom to advantage, employing every trick they know to infiltrate the interior; they ask to use the lavatory or for a glass of water to help swallow a vital pill (prompting concern in the helpers which might be useful later); they request leave to deposit their shopping trolleys somewhere safe in the building, and beg for chairs to rest their weary bones while they wait. Of course, they insist, they wouldn't dream of stopping anybody from working – they know the helpers must all be *so* busy – so they'll collect the chairs themselves, and as they pass the more interesting stalls, their trained eyes are taking in everything. If they are quiet and careful they might even be forgotten for a few moments and allowed to potter a little, to the chagrin of those waiting outside. And if a helper shows any friendliness he or she may be asked to put by some choice item – appealed to on the grounds that, as pensioners, they can't afford to buy new things, and with their wobbly old pins they may even have trouble getting to and around the trestles (an artistic stagger goes down well at this point). Eventually, these 'gentle' creatures are comfortably seated outside the door – but when it comes to the Great Rush, just watch their poor old legs shift!

Meanwhile, jumblers who can't claim the dubious perks of seniority have to content themselves with being as helpful as possible with the incoming jumble, and hope that rushing to open doors and offering to carry bags will allow a few seconds' closer glimpse of the stalls; some canny practitioners even come equipped with a bag of jumble to donate as a passport to this small privilege, while everyone secretly longs to be invited in to help with the sorting.

During the Great Rush most jumblers will want to follow – or beat – the leaders to the White Elephant stall, because thereon reposes the dream of that once-in-a-lifetime bargain. If this is to be *the* jumble sale, it is on that trestle that the Cartier watch will nestle unrecognised – or the Ming vase, the Turner sketch, the diamond necklace (so vividly vulgar no one but you guesses it can be real), the jade carving, the heavy gold brooch, the seventeenth-century glass beaker, the Dresden figurine, the rare medal . . . but simply because the field of what might be valuable is *so* wide, by necessity the dream, though ever recurrent, is vague. Unless fulfilled, it will be dispelled each time by the hard fact that less valuable yet still worthwhile objects are *actually* to be seen on the trestle – and you can, with a sneaking feeling of relief, put aside the dream until next time.

Some jumblers have a different dream. These people are the specialist collectors who know a great deal about, say, books or records and for them heaven would be to find a rare first edition or disc; they may not be jumble-bugs as such, just addicted to increasing their collections and using jumble sales as another possible means to do this. Other people are more pragmatic and may go in with a firm resolve to buy a good winter coat or a pair of shoes. They will make for the stalls that are important to them, and will have a few blessed minutes to browse before the hordes have picked clean the White Elephant and dispersed to whatever attracts them next.

You must decide what your priorities are and weigh up the chances of getting anywhere near a bargain amongst the possibly more skilled, more knowledgeable, more ruthless jumblophiles of long standing. Perhaps a good-as-new duvet cover and five double damask dinner napkins on Household Linens would be pleasing enough bargains to make you forget what might have been had you joined the throng around the bric-à-brac.

## How to Shop

Before you bridle and think 'I've done more shopping than she's had hot dinners', I must point out that jumbling is unlike any other shopping except, perhaps, the opening five minutes of Harrods' January sale. Many people miss so much by not realising that they have to apply a totally different technique.

To begin with there is no time for hesitancy. Every decision has to be snap and each one must follow hard on the heels of the other. Your eyes must be everywhere, for bargains are to be had, not just on the trestle but also on the floor in front of it, in boxes at the end or underneath, and even on a ledge or stage behind.

As no two items are likely to be the same, *everything* needs to be inspected – which means that it is no good breaking through the crowd at one point, having a cursory look at the goods in front of you, then withdrawing to try the same tactic on the next table. Once you have secured a place at the table's edge you must be prepared to hang on to it and aim to slide yourself along, inspecting everything as you go. And that means picking up things both to look at and to see what's lurking beneath; there must be no expectations of neatness or logic on a jumble stall (especially the White Elephant) and small items are likely to be hiding under or behind large ones. Containers should be looked into to see if other things have been wrapped up and popped inside for safe transportation, then forgotten, while piles of flattish objects should be sifted through right to the bottom in case a pretty plate has found its way between the plain ones. Remember, in the pre-sale sort-out many helpers are feeding items onto the stall, usually in a great hurry, and with little thought other than to get them into the appropriate general area. Moreover, many quite experienced helpers believe it to be a waste of time to arrange their stock tidily or logically as the customers will reduce it to chaos in ten seconds flat!

A timid nature and proper up-bringing must certainly be rejected. It's not a good idea to ask your neighbour to 'pass the cruet': he might decide to buy it himself! A long arm must be made; for it is tacitly accepted amongst jumble-bugs that your part of the table is as far as you can reach on either side, and if you see something further off that you like the look of, attract the helper's attention and ask her to hand it to you. To repeat the advice offered to helpers in Chapter Ten: *never ask how much it is until you have it firmly in your hands*; it may until now have escaped the notice of someone much closer to it, or they may have seen it but assumed the cost to be too high until the helper gives you a price – then, suddenly, it's not there for you to buy any more. And if you're doubtful whether you really want something or not, keep it in your hand until you have made a firm decision; if you don't, it's a pound to a penny that the second your fingers relinquish hold of it another's will curl round in proud possession and you will know with dreadful certainty that the decision you made was *wrong*.

Sometimes the person to the side of you may seem set in concrete and has no intention of moving from the spot, deeply ruminating on the finer points of a slightly chipped

*Jumble sales are a body-contact sport . . .*

99

Chinese vase that he or she is turning over; you will *have* to give up your place to get round such blockages. Slide round behind them and wait the second or two it takes to break in through a gap as near to where you left off as possible. Jumbling is most definitely a body-contact sport and as such calls on you to practise the very un-English behaviour of pushing your body closer to that of a stranger than would normally be thought polite. Don't worry, so long as you keep your hands on the table, your close proximity will hardly impinge upon the other's deep concentration – with a little luck just far enough to make them absent-mindedly squash up a bit to allow you some room.

Your money supply should be securely zipped away in pocket or bag. Don't be in too much of a hurry to pull it out and expose it, especially while you are picking up and putting down objects you might or might not want to buy. How easy it is to find yourself puzzling, 'Why am I still holding this loathsome, cracked egg-cup?' – followed by a horrified 'And where's my purse?' The point must also be made that every minute spent attracting a helper's attention, enquiring about the price and then sorting through your small change, is a lost opportunity for finding another bargain before it falls into someone else's hands.

Ideally, it is best to gather everything in one arm and pay for it all together, once you are sure you've checked over the entire stall; but this is not always practical. Sometimes the articles are too large or too unwieldy for you to hold on to for long and this is when you must apply tactics; you must identify the most amenable helper.

While your concentration has seemingly been devoted to the inspection of jumble, your ears and part of your mind should have been heeding the conversations around you, notably those referring to money. As you browse from helper to helper you may become aware that one of them seems to be asking very little and another a lot; you form a general impression that, while in one place pennies are tentatively suggested, in the other pounds are stridently demanded. Without breaking your concentration to discover the goods to which the prices might apply, browse towards the helper with the most pleasing attitude and give her a big smile.

If she – or he – seems approachable and the area behind the stall is not particularly open to other customers (more of which later), you can try one of two techniques: either request a price and pay for your armful of goods there and then, put them in a bag and ask her to look after it for you; or suggest that she simply takes charge of your collection so far, and anything else you choose will be passed back to her to be added to the pile, and you will pay for the lot in one go. Both methods have the advantage of leaving you with arms free, while your chosen break-ables are safer behind the stall than they are dangling in a carrier-bag from your wrist, clashing with others' similar appendages and hampering your efforts at sorting.

However, to perfect these techniques there are some precautions you must take; what you do *not* want is your bag or collection of jumble to be handed over to someone else, either in error or at the plausible request of a petty thief! Remember, one supermarket carrier-bag looks pretty much like another, and if a helper is very busy the customers can be just as unmemorable. So when you smile brightly at your chosen helper, make sure she notices you particularly; say something to make her remember you, be wearing something bright on your top half that she can't fail to notice, and establish a connection between you and your purchases. If your collection is to be put aside unbagged, make a witticism about one of the objects so she connects it with you, then when you are further along the table and want to send more things back to the pile, you can ask for them to be put with 'the pineapple' or 'the backscratcher', etc. If your goods are already paid for and put aside bagged, it is a good idea to come prepared with carriers bearing your name written in thick felt-tip pen just *inside* the top, or with your name printed on slips of paper to tuck into every full bag – the idea being that the identification is visible to the helper but not to the opportunist criminal standing next to you, who could use the knowledge to strengthen his or her false claim to your purchases.

Sometimes the tables are placed in such a way that there is no room for storage of bags, or the stalls are open on all sides to customers and anything left with a helper could disappear the moment she turns her head away. In these cases you are forced to keep your bags with you; put them on the ground between your legs where they will be fairly well protected and won't hamper your arm movements, then when you've finished on that particular stall, look for another – better positioned – where they can safely take charge of your purchases. If all else fails and you haven't a car parked conveniently outside while your collection of goodies grows out of hand, ask for a tall cardboard box, stuff your bags inside and drag it around the floor, keeping it under the trestle just in front of you as you sort through the remaining jumble. And if they can't provide a cardboard box, you'll just have to give up and go home. If you've got that many bulky bags to deal with you've probably bought enough anyway!

Whatever technique you use you may find a helper regarding you with suspicion, especially whilst you're gathering together a collection of items; in the past he or she may have been tricked by customers who use an armful as cover to slip other items into their bags, have simply walked out without paying or have expected a ridiculously reduced price for 'buying in bulk'. This person may have a vague uneasiness at the thought of anyone bothering to shop with method at a jumble sale, so, even having taken your money, he or she will still feel somehow diddled – in which case friendly overtures just heighten suspicion. If one of this sort challenges you simply because you are holding a string of beads and a glass tumbler in your left hand whilst you reach for an interesting bag of bits with your right, accept the inevitable, pay up and don't bother asking for 'favours'. Such a helper will consider even a request that he or she looks after your paid-for purchases to have a catch in it; she doesn't know how, but she's sure it's a ploy to get away with something.

Assuming, for now, that all has gone smoothly on the White Elephant stall, you are about to move on, and a friendly helper has agreed to look after your bargains. Make sure that your bag has been placed *safely*, not at the end of the stall where people pass by, and *never under the table* where it can be taken for unsorted jumble and be sold all over again. This applies wherever in the hall you leave whatever sort of jumble, but most especially to the stuff you buy on the White Elephant, which is more likely to be lost to a thief. Every time you have finished sorting another stall, pop back to the first one to check your bags are still there; it will only take a second yet will keep your face known to the helpers – not just the one who agreed to look after your bags, but any others on the stall, for who's to say when your chosen helper might go walkabout, leaving a newcomer in charge?

I think I should point out that crime and accident are not as frequent as it may seem here, where one person's experiences of mayhem, originally lightly sprinkled throughout twenty-five years of ardent jumbling, have been lumped together. If you were to go into an old-fashioned country garden where the summer flowers all merge in a riot of colour and perfume, yet you picked only the smallest, dullest weeds, the resulting bunch could not be thought a fair representation of that garden. So it is with jumble sales; if petty thieving and carelessness are the weeds, the flowers are the excitement beforehand, the thrill of spotting a bargain and beating your neighbour to it and the continuing enjoyment of it when you take it home – exotic blooms indeed, and bigger and brighter where the gardener tends his patch with knowledge and imagination.

There is no doubt that going to jumble sales is an exhausting pastime. Physically, turning over piles of jumble, bending and straightening, holding your arms out in front of you for minutes on end can be very tiring and it makes sense to use any tips you can get on how to make it easier. No less exhausting is the speed at which the brain has to work to get the best out of jumbling, and here, too, there are methods that simplify the process, speed up the reactions and make you smugly confident that you are getting more out of your hobby than most of your colleagues.

Before you go into a sale, clear your mind of preconceived ideas of what you want. If you go looking for a grey cardigan you may subconsciously reject a pretty blue sweater, even though a second's detached thought would tell you that it might well match another outfit in your wardrobe. Your intellect, happiest with a very few concepts at a time, will latch onto the twin ideas of 'grey' and 'cardigan' and will reject so quickly anything that doesn't fit those criteria that you may not be aware you've even picked up – and put down – a blue sweater at all. Better by far to learn to appreciate the wider concept of quality – quality in all its forms, be it on the White Elephant, Book, Clothing or Cake stalls. The antique dealer Lovejoy, in Jonathan Gash's books and on television, talks of being a 'divi' (a contraction of 'diviner') and says that the moment he sees, or touches a genuine antique he gets a 'boing!' in his chest, a breathless excitement that is a sure indication of the worth of the object that prompted such a reaction. There is no reason why that 'sixth sense' shouldn't react to anything of good quality that has found its way onto a jumble sale stall, and no reason why anyone who really wants to can't train themselves to be that sensitive.

Imagine yourself at a Clothing stall, working at speed, plunging your hand in and out of a mixed pile of polyester, viscose and acrylic garments, instantly – almost automatically – rejecting on sight nine-tenths of what you pull out . . . but then your fingers touch pure silk or cashmere (the warmest of wools) and there in your chest is the 'boing!' of recognition, the breathlessness of rising excitement and the heady feeling as the adrenalin begins to pump – the certainty that you are about to pull out something special! But you have to be able to recognise such fibres before you can do that. Looking at the label is a sweet, triumphant confirmation and can give an extra thrill if an expensive name is revealed, heightened again by a shrewd assessment of how much the garment originally cost.

Training yourself to a degree of discernment need not involve hours of study, nor even disrupt your day-to-day life, but can be an occasional, sensuously pleasurable occupation. Simply, whenever you have a moment or two whilst shopping in town, make a point of handling any clothes for sale that are attractive to you; this way you will learn the feel of different fabrics. Try to identify the cloth from touch and colour alone before you look at the label or read the price. Compare the way different materials handle; crumple a corner of the garment in your hand and see if it springs back or stays creased, then read the washing or cleaning instructions. The fact that you shop at jumble sales is no reason to be a slave to the sink and ironing-board.

And, while your finger-tips are learning to touch, your eyes must learn not to be dazzled by bright colours. Generally speaking, the more garish the tone, the cheaper the fabric; good, glowing colours can look positively washed out alongside cheap, bright, harsh polyester. Yet hold them out on their own and you can see their richness and subtlety. Faded cotton can be attractive when ironed, yet may be totally overlooked when screwed in a ball on the trestle – go for the quality of the cotton, be it a fine lawn or a thick chambray, using your eyes to check that the weave is dense and even, and the hands to feel for soft, smooth suppleness. The quality of man-made fabrics is just as wide-ranging and some designer garments in acrylic or viscose can cost as much as silk or wool when new, yet be easier to take care of. Teach yourself to recognise these in just the same way, by sight and touch.

However, it's not enough to buy something because it's the right material (unless you plan to resell it . . . or have read the next chapter of this book); it has to be the right size and style. Size is easy; if the label's missing, a tape measure run from side seam to side seam will give you roughly half the chest, waist or hip measurement; but about style you will have to learn to be strong-willed. Accept right from the beginning that there is no way you can dress from jumble sales and *follow* fashion – except from a very long distance. Even if someone buys a brand-new, up-to-the-minute dress and hates it as soon as she gets it home, it's unlikely that she'll put it in a jumble sale as soon as a week later; most clothing is at least out of fashion before it's given away, and some of it can have spent decades at the back of a wardrobe. But this gives you a unique opportunity; once you have shaken off the shackles of the 'fickle fashion' columns in the women's magazines you are free to take inspiration from any era, and to put together the look that really suits *you*. After all, that's nothing more or less than the designers do!

Begin by evaluating your current wardrobe, and take a long, hard look at the clothes that give you pleasure, or otherwise, in the wearing; never mind how much you paid for it, does that skirt make you itch or does that dress ride up and need pulling down all the time. And although that green colour was all the rage a while ago, does it make your skin look sallow and dirty? Do you wear that skirt so much because it's *exactly* the right length to show off your legs to perfection, or the other one because you like the feel of its soft, billowy fullness around you? From this exercise you will learn which materials you like to feel against your skin, which colours suit you and which ones you should avoid like the plague; which styles hide full hips, a wobbly bottom, top-heavy bust or whatever you find unpleasing in your construction, and which ones accentuate your good points. With that dossier of facts learnt by heart, when you go jumbling you should be able automatically to pull out of the pile on the trestle anything that fits the correct criteria.

After a while you will find yourself absorbing similar details about family and friends, and will get almost as much pleasure recognising something exactly right – size, style, colour and cloth – for a neighbour three doors down as you do in buying for yourself; just exercising such a skill can be satisfying, like finishing the *Times* crossword in ten minutes! Instead of the usual eleven and a half.

Of course, an open mind can't fail to be aware of current fashion trends, some of which will be instantly attractive. By all means keep an eye on shop windows and try on the new styles occasionally, then when you find something similar on the trestles you will know whether to buy it or not. You don't have to be stuck in a rut, or stay in pleated skirts for ever because that's what suited you on the day you investigated your wardrobe.

When you are used to jumble shopping you may ponder on how tempting and how right for you the rails of brand-new clothes in a shop may seem – until you take examples into the changing room and put them on to discover that a dropped waistline makes you look as if you're walking on your knees, or this season's 'singing tones' are tone deaf on you; which would be depressing if you were really looking for a new outfit. And you may gloat over the number of times you have pulled a scrap of cloth from amongst others tumbled on a trestle, peered at it in the gloom of a village hall and decided to buy it in careless haste (no trying it on in a roomful of others, feeling slightly ashamed of your serviceable white knickers and the flab around them; no long and painful deliberations) only to find it fits you perfectly and makes you look like a million dollars!

Jumble skills are not exclusive to the Clothing stalls. At the White Elephant so many people are locked into ideas of antiques, collectables and china that their eyes don't see such other things as cosmetics and toiletries. Granted, used lipstick and eye make-up are to be avoided because of the germs they may carry, but it is hard to imagine how tubes of face cream or bottles of shampoo could be contaminated in the normal run of things; and one would have to be very unlucky indeed to become the victim of a joker who would lace a pot of face cream with something nasty. Perfectly wholesome, expensive toiletries tend to be given for sale when people can't think of anything else to hand over to the enthusiastic jumble collector waiting on the doorstep. You can do well to cash in on such generosity. If you are consistently lucky in picking up face creams and powders, soaps, shampoo and conditioners for a few pennies at a time, then you can put the money you save towards a large bottle of your favourite, expensive perfume.

The fun of jumbling is not restricted to attending the sales themselves; a lot of secret amusement can be had by sweeping into a superior establishment to buy one of their exclusive fragrances, knowing that you are dressed from head to foot in the more elegant of your jumble purchases (the lot probably costing less than £1!), and looking better than anyone else in the place.

What your eye sees and what your brain makes of the items on the White Elephant is where skill tells: a bottle brush with an unusually long handle may be just the right size to clean that coffee-pot with an awkward spout; a Horlicks mixing glass and plunger, *circa* 1950s, the kids can use for making frothy milk-shakes; and a round or oval vanity case, long superseded as a fashion accessory by the more casual airline bag, makes an excellent hat box at a time when hats are coming back into fashion but suitable receptacles are hard to find, and cost the earth! Never let your mind – or your hand – pass over something it doesn't recognise immediately, but be curious and worry at whatever it is; when light dawns you will have the advantage over those with closed, incurious intellects. Take Anne, for instance, who saw a slightly familiar piece of metal at one end of the stall, and came across another, similar piece further along. The helper was surprised when Anne put the two together, *her* mind not having registered them as halves of a whole. She was amazed that this loony customer actually wanted to buy something that was obviously broken – and so dumbfounded she could only bring herself to ask five pence for it! Anne now boasts the best designed, efficient and easy-to-clean garlic press in the Western world – one of those marvellous gadgets that's praised to the skies in magazines, yet impossible to find in the shops.

Then there's Jean, who spotted something unusual and carefully worked out what it was to gain herself a useful kitchen antique. Recognising the piece as of the same china as Victorian pudding basins, which she knows are collectable, she picked it up and held onto it whilst part of her mind puzzled what use a shallow china cone with a slit in the side could possibly have. With luck it wouldn't be identified as the only remaining unsmashed part of a more complex article. Meanwhile, she carried on inspecting the goods on the stall until she was satisfied she had the answer. The helper from whom she asked the price was intrigued, but Jean made sure she had handed over the money and that the 'thing' belonged to her before she disclosed that it was a Victorian egg-separator – a very wise move as it turned out, for the helper tried to snatch it back, no doubt vexed at her own dull-wittedness and disappointed that she hadn't kept it for herself. And now, every time a recipe calls for the white of egg, Jean giggles at the thought of that cross helper and gives a smug little smile as she uses her unusual antique.

## Practicalities

While your brain is working on many planes – identifying mysterious objects, remembering sizes and styles and contemplating a thousand and one things – on one plane it must coolly check each chosen article for damage; and as speed is as important in this as in any other decisions whilst jumbling, it obviously helps to know beforehand which areas are most likely to bear evidence of wear and tear. Take a china teapot: spout, lid and handle are the bits that protrude or drop out in daily use and will be the first to show rough handling; if they are in good order, then it's worth taking a little extra time to look inside the pot. That's just common sense, but other lessons are learnt through bitter experience. Someone who reaches the climax of a jumble-bought paperback, only to find the last pages missing, does tend, when buying a book thereafter, to flick through to check it's intact before handing over hard cash.

In this respect, despite previous mention, jigsaw puzzles are worth another two paragraphs all of their own. Many people are fervently addicted to putting together tiny pasteboard scraps, and the jumble sale is an excellent source of what is otherwise a very expensive pastime. Some jigsaws appear on the Book or Toy stalls as pristine as when they were displayed in the shop, and with modern wall-to-wall carpets there is less chance of pieces being lost between floor boards or slipping out of sight under lino squares, but there can be no guarantee that the puzzle you buy will be complete and undamaged. However, careful investigation will give some indication of condition. To begin with, be particularly wary of open boxes with the pieces loose inside; buy this jigsaw only if there is none better and you can't bear a Saturday evening twiddling your thumbs – there's far more chance of a few of its pieces having gone astray in transportation and the jumble sort-out than in normal use. A box sealed on two or four sides with sellotape does show forethought on someone's part, but that might have been the helper who came across it upturned on the floor, and hastily thrust back as many pieces as could be found! And a taped box doesn't allow you to see the quality of the cardboard or the printing of the picture; nor whether it's been damp at some point and the card and paper have parted company.

Ideally, the box should be unbroken and bright; if it's faded the picture on the lid may differ too much from that on the puzzle. The pieces should be in a clear plastic bag, with extra Brownie points if it's the original cellophane, showing that someone has looked after it from the beginning. Lastly, before you buy you should look through the plastic bag at a representative selection of the plain cardboard backs of the pieces. If some of these are a different colour, and the picture on the box has a large expanse of plain colour (almost inevitably sky), you can guess that the puzzle was kept as 'work in progress' in front of a window for a number of days, also that the sky proved tedious so was left until last with the pieces scattered in the sunlight. When *you* come to do this area it will prove almost impossible because, with some pieces faded and others not, colour matching will be hopelessly restricted. This may seem a minor point, but not when you have already spent five hours working on the puzzle and just want to see it finished.

The items on the Clothing and Household Linen stalls are likely to number more than twice the pieces of the jigsaw puzzle you have just bought, and each one must be checked for stains, tears and worn patches as swiftly as possible: a daunting task if you haven't learned to make that process automatic. And if the quantity of jumble is truly immense, even the most skilled and experienced jumble-bug might retire, hurt and bewildered, half-way through.

Check Household Linens first, where you may find anything from a king-sized terylene or duck-down duvet (with cover) through curtains, sheets and tablecloths down to serviceable table napkins. A duvet is worth having, even if it's only to use as a rug for children to play on, or as a wrap for a sick person. Cleaning it needn't be a worry. Look for the label at one corner: if you can make out the instructions on it, well and good; if it's floppy and unreadable then that indicates it has been often washed,

ergo the duvet has to be washable; and if there's no label, stop at the nearest dry cleaning shop on the way home and ask their advice. Even if you have to spend a few pounds on having it professionally laundered it will probably be worthwhile.

The last point holds true for curtains and even blankets, if what you find on the trestle fits your need. With the former, look for fading and make sure, by giving discoloured bits a good hard tug, that the material hasn't rotted; 'antique' curtains can sometimes be found, and look lovely used as an ornamental feature, rather than as working, drawable drapes. If the colours don't run (a good test is to dampen a corner and rub in a little soap) it may be safest to wash them, spread out in the bath, with a light, gentle pressing action, then agitate them in clean water to rinse, and finally take them, evenly folded, to an area where they can be allowed to dry spread out flat. Dry cleaning would be too harsh a treatment for something so fragile.

Ask the helper to hold up blankets so you can see any stains or wear in the centre. Feather pillows must be in extraordinarily good condition before they should be considered, and even washable man-made-fibre pillow pads may have hopelessly stained covers – not pleasant to have against your cheek all night.

Little gems of lace may be found trimming old linen tablecloths, while hand-embroidered chair-backs can be nice enough to frame and display on the wall. Nowadays, rust marks are removable from white linen with a preparation from the range of 'Stain Devils' to be found in good hardware shops, so don't let that sort of damage put you off buying otherwise attractive napery. My own dinner table is usually decked with sparkling white linen napkins, which are very often hot-washed and starched stiff as soldiers; with such treatment they do tend to wear thin, but I can normally replace them from jumble sales, finding the most beautiful woven damask patterns that date from a time when everyone used napkins and table-cloths (pre-formica table tops), and shops carried a selection of designs. One such napkin, surprisingly, on close inspection proved to be an intricately woven portrait of John Wesley!

Quickly cast an eye over Shoes (which speak for themselves) and Nearly New, where you may be hopeful that checking for wear and tear has already been done for you (and is reflected in the higher price), then it's on to Clothing. Start at one end of the stall. Most jumble sale organisers do their best to have apparel sorted into ladies', gentlemen's and children's; if you want ladies' clothing and the end where you've wormed your way in is the children's section, then work your way out pretty smartly, go to the other end of the row of trestles and start again. If you first come across gents' clothing, stay where you are and begin to sort your way through it; as a section on its own it won't occupy a great length of trestle and there are usually a lot of ladies' clothes mixed up amongst the shirts, suits and pyjamas.

If you work to the method of passing goods to a helper to look after until you decide to pay for them, you will have two opportunities to check the clothes for damage (given you are not about to dash off to another sale, that is, and thus won't be able to spare the time). As you begin to pluck your chosen articles and either tuck them under one arm or drape them over your shoulders while you listen out for the most amenable helper, you must give the clothes a quick inspection. Later, when you have chosen your helper and she has amassed everything you have sent back to her from one end of the line to the other, then you can have a more leisurely sort through and 'prune' your pile – an especially good idea when garments destined for someone else's heap might have been misdirected onto yours, and vice versa. So if that little silk number you were particularly pleased to lay your hands on seems to have gone missing en route, a search can be instigated amongst the other put-by piles. Then again, there's always the chance that any old things may have fallen off the trestle and been kicked onto your pile: very vexing when on arriving home you find them and realise you paid extra for the privilege!

Like teapots, clothes have areas that suffer more strain than others, and it is better to be able to discard something at first glance than to get it home and be disappointed to find a large hole in the elbow.

## Shirts and Blouses

Begin with the inside of the collar, then check the front for stains, look at the elbows, then see if someone with too broad a back has worn it and stretched almost to breaking point the stitches attaching the sleeves.

## Jumpers and Cardigans

Elbows are most vulnerable and, if not actually holed, may be thin. After inspecting them, check for broken threads along the cuff, neckline and bottom edges and, holding the garment up to the light, for moth holes. If all's well so far, then a woolly may have been thrown out because of a stubborn stain; look at it carefully in good light.

## Sweatshirts

These casual yet hard-wearing garments are normally worn to extinction, so if you find a fairly new one on the trestle, be suspicious. If you're lucky it will have been abandoned merely because it didn't fit, but it could have been ruined by a deep-seated stain. Check the label immediately: if it's a cotton–polyester mix that could spell trouble since it is a material that clings to grease with tenacity; cotton on its own is at least boilable.

Should the sweatshirt prove to be stain-free, carry on inspecting it as for jumpers.

## Trousers

Unless you positively enjoy replacing zips, never buy trousers, and especially tough denims, with either a broken zip or one that looks likely to break in the near future. Peer inside the garment for worn pockets or stains at the crotch, then look along the outside front of each leg for marks and wear at the knees – you may realise as your eye moves down that the width of the trousers is so much the antithesis of current fashion that you instantly abandon them. If not, see that the backside is not worn, shiny or bagged before committing yourself.

## Skirts

A casual, unstructured skirt should be checked for the state of the zip, for staining and to make sure that any elastic at the waist hasn't perished. For a formal skirt, where an excellent cut is important to give a smooth, flattering line, inspecting the label is a good initial move. If you get a 'boing!' of recognition at the touch of the material which is borne out by reading on the label that the skirt is made of pure wool by a name such as Jaeger then you can buy with confidence. And, if further investigation shows invisible hemming, a good-quality lining unfrayed at the seams and a firm waistband then you can forgive a broken zip; this garment will more than adequately reward the cost of professional mending and cleaning by looking good and feeling comfortable in wear for many years to come. If the label is not so impressive and the skirt has no lining, be very wary; it may be that the wool is unbearably itchy, even through a petticoat. Other problems to look out for are a baggy seat and a lining that's drooped below the hemline.

## Overcoats

Here again the cut is all-important. Cheaper coats with lean and skimped material do not age gracefully and have a habit of looking sadly worn and dated; once the lining has gone, especially under the arms, they lose their shape very quickly. A good, full-skirted trench-coat (look out for a Burberry with its distinctive plaid lining) or a classic black, navy or camel coat can be a welcome addition to your wardrobe and will probably last for ever, as long as there are no immovable stains or any fraying at collar and cuff.

## Anoraks

Check the lining as for overcoats, then any zips and the condition of the material under the arms where sweat might have left its mark. Make sure the anorak is washable.

## Underwear

Remember, you have put away squeamishness; so if you don't reject the thought of jumble undies out of hand you may be in for a pleasant surprise. Most people begin with the high ideal that they draw the line at jumble bras and pants – until they bother to inspect some pretty, frothy article and find it looking exactly as it did when it came from the shop. And what can possibly be wrong with a garment that has no stains and no signs of wear? The likelihood is that it was bought for a lady too embarrassed at not fitting into it or feeling uncomfortable in it to take it back to the shop, so she kept it until it was forgotten by the giver and slipped it into the pile of jumble, probably relieved to be rid of something that acted as a mute reproach every time she opened her drawer.

Examine the elastic underarms of bras for marks or perishing, check the hooks and eyes for stress and around the cups for broken or missing bones.

With any clothes you buy, the label is a good indication of quality and condition. If it is uncreased and unmarked, the garment is as near to brand new as makes no difference, but if it's faded and floppy then it has been through the washing machine a good few times. There again, if the tag itself is made of high-quality material, is expertly and attractively designed with the words woven rather than printed and is sewn on by hand with tiny stitches at each corner, then you can be confident that the garment it graces is something worth having. Labels that are cut out, cut through or starred with indelible pen generally indicate the clothes are 'seconds' and might be flawed – possibly faded display models. A scratchy, reinforced paper tag stamped with a number indicates that the article came from a catalogue.

Be wary of any material that is badly creased, for it has either been shamefully treated in the wash and will be impossible to flatten, or is the kind of cloth that will need constant attention. Likewise steer away from knitted garments that have 'pilled' unless you have an electric gadget to remove those nasty little bobbles (very prevalent under the arms, by the way). If a jumper's label says size sixteen and your judgement tells you it's size twelve, then cast it back, for shrunken woollies never have the suppleness, the draping quality and the warmth of the unshrunken.

Unless you have a penchant for altering clothes and have years of experience of, say, turning a dress into a blouse and skirt or adding inserts to make the dress two sizes larger, don't be tempted to buy clothes with that idea in mind. The nearest you should come to it is when you know you will have to take up a hem (not let one down, it always shows). Although you may have the best intentions you'll find that the dress, or whatever, is soon forgotten in favour of the many jumble clothes that do fit without alteration. I once made the claim that I had fifty shirts and blouses in my wardrobe; being a truthful person I then counted them and was amazed to find ninety-five hanging there, all but two the outcome of years of jumbling and probably costing no more than £9 the lot! With all those to choose from, why should I buy clothes that need altering? You may soon reach a similar conclusion and also, as I have done, refine your shopping even further just to cut down the sheer bulk of what you bring home. When your stock of pure wool sweaters gets out of hand you may decide only to buy machine-washable pure wool, or even just cashmere!

And finally, as the last in this list of shopping hints, while you shuffle along the trestles don't be scornful of what falls on the floor and gets under your feet. There is as much likelihood of a Bruce Oldfield creation being down there as up on the table.

# CHAPTER THIRTEEN

## . . . And How to be Brilliant!

So you've taken to heart the lessons of the previous chapter and now regularly arrive home from jumbling forays with a good selection of quality clothing, books and bric-à-brac. Not only are you exhilarated by the excitement of the sale, but you are thrilled when the bargains you have found for husband, teenage daughter and neighbour three doors down meet with rapturous approval. It should be enough. But. . . .

Time after time as you stand at the trestle you spot a glint of something special, a flash of gorgeous colour, and know immediately that you want whatever it is with all your heart; then you pull it out and find it is completely the wrong size, woefully out of fashion or damaged in some way. Even a fairly skilled jumbler could believe there's nothing for it but to cast the article back like an undersized trout, with as much regret as the fisherman who was hoping for a good breakfast; but it hurts to have your instinct baulked, and you watch with regret as the rich fabric is swallowed up by the river of drab cast-offs.

Lateral thinking can change all that. As a concept it has been around a long time: the man who invented the wheel was a lateral thinker, as were the women coping with war-time shortages who drew lines up the back of their legs to imitate stocking seams. The phrase itself was only coined by Edward de Bono in the 1960s. A lateral thinker at a jumble sale will pick up a rich velvet or brocade curtain and not be at all put out that its mate is nowhere to be seen, for her mind has moved smartly away from the fixed idea that the material must flank a window (which is where other minds stop short) and visualised instead the glowing colours as cushion covers; and there are few limitations to the successive sideways hops her imagination might take thereafter.

If she is no hand at a needle the curtain, ready hemmed and edged as it is, may dress an unsightly radiator to camouflage it during the summer, or, draped, bunched and discreetly pinned into place over a pole, may make a striking pelmet for contrasting plain curtains. She can use it to cover shelves or the back of a glass-fronted cupboard simply by stapling it in place and gluing braid around the edge to hide the staples – a technique that can also be used to decorate the back wall of an alcove or niche, as long as battens to take the staples are nailed to the wall first. More ambitiously, an old, panelled door may be glamorised if the curtain, cut to fit the panels and padded with wadding, is stapled into place (or if the wooden moulding around each panel is taken out, then replaced over the raw edge of the material, thus holding it securely). The centre of each panel can then be studded, with either a brass stud or a fabric-covered button. A bed-head could be padded in the same way.

A good needlewoman can make of a single curtain a range of bags, from shopping holdall and knitting reticule sizes down to make-up purse and spectacles case – perhaps for sale at the village fête or to be given as Christmas presents. Another effective yet easy-to-sew article along those lines is the roll: a length of material padded, lined and fitted with elasticated loops specifically to hold such things as knitting pins, crochet hooks or jewellery, which can be rolled up and tied into place.

Then there are some rather spectacular clothes that can be made from a curtain by a competent seamstress by the simple addition of lining, fixings and trimmings – perhaps buttons and zips gleaned from other jumble sales. How about a sumptuous brocade waistcoat or evening skirt, or a flowing velvet cape?

And, given a big enough curtain, a loose cover can be fashioned for an armchair, or seat covers for a dining suite . . . but our lateral thinker may have taken an even larger sideways leap. She may be collecting a whole load of mixed brocade or velvet curtains with one aim in mind. Perhaps she can't afford a replacement for her dilapidated old sofa, or wants something to protect it from over-indulged pets, and has found that draping it with a collection of curtains (rufflette headings removed and edges neatened) can give a relaxed yet opulent impression. Carried out in red brocades and velvets ranging from deep plum through crimson to scarlet, the various colours, far from clashing, give the sofa the look of an Indian palan-quin or a Turkish ottoman (in the true sense of the word and not, as it has come to mean, a blanket chest). The more tones of red the better, for if two or three overlapping look a careless mismatch, a lot of them together are a bold statement; and if some of the brocades have gold or blue woven in, the final result is so much more interesting. A very different, 'garden' effect can be created, using cotton chintz or linen union flower prints with soft cream and green backgrounds, and an occasional plain pastel cushion for contrast.

There are two ways in which to achieve this sort of renovation, the easier yet less permanent being to drape the curtains one by one over the back and arms of the sofa (or armchair). Make sure that the best part of one covers the worn and faded part of another and ruche them a little; then, using one long curtain to cover all the seat cushions, tuck in the excess along the back and sides, ensuring the front edge falls in a neat, straight line to the floor; add scatter cushions to enhance the look of padded comfort. The second way involves sewing most of the curtains together in a long strip that, loosely gathered, completely shrouds the back and arms; another piece should be tacked along the front of the sofa and separate covers made for the seat cushions. Using either method of construction, the gathered drapes will need occasional refreshing – a good shake out and regathering to form soft folds instead of sharp pressed creases. And if any of the curtains becomes too disreputable even to be hidden away among the better bits, then replace it with another. Jumble-bought, of course.

113

These are just a few ideas for single curtains, and no doubt there are many more. Heaven forbid that they should flash across the mind all at once as you stand at the trestle, fingering the material! No, it is enough that you are strongly attracted to the article and want to see it fulfil some role in your home; once you are confident of your ability to think laterally you will look forward to musing over various ingenious ideas for a bargain's employment. There's immense pleasure to be had in a small success that demonstrates how clever you can be.

If you can add another decorative improvisation to your original notion, so much the better. Try intertwining jumble-found tassels and cords (discarded tie-backs or even silky dressing-gown cords) with the bunched and draped material of your pelmet, or use them to trim the edges of cushion covers, tied in a bow at one corner with the tassels hanging loose. For the draped sofa idea, if you draw the material into a bunch at the corners or at the front of the arms then bind with the cord, you can give your 'make do and mend' renovation the look of expensive designer treatment. Follow the theme through with tassels and cords draped over framed pictures on the wall, around a lampshade or looped over the newel post on the staircase, and put by the biggest, fattest, shiniest ones for weaving into Christmas garlands (tie them in bows where the garlands are looped); their sheen is richer and far more opulent than that of mass-produced baubles and ties made for the purpose.

Articles on the White Elephant stall are not exempt from the lateral thinker's attention. That nice picture frame without any glass can surround a rectangle of painted softboard or cork tiles and, hey presto, a rather superior notice-board. Criss-cross it with thin ribbon or black elastic and you have something reminiscent of the board in the entrance hall to an old-fashioned gentlemen's club. A bag of brightly coloured plastic clothes pegs can prompt a brainwave, as they did for Mary, who loves telling people how she uses them to secure the tops of cereal packets and other soft packaged dry goods in her larder, and how they stop her vegetables from spilling all over the floor of the freezer. When you see for sale purpose-made clips, expensively shrink-wrapped in pairs on their cardboard backing but designed on exactly the same principle as the humble peg, you have to admit Mary has a point.

Even a battered old sieve can be put to a very decorative use. Wedge a lump of dry oasis block inside (it doesn't have to fit perfectly) then build up a half-ball posy shape by pushing dried flower and grass stems through the wires into the block; bind the handle of the sieve with toning ribbon and use it to hang the arrangement. A succession of these in different sizes on a staircase wall looks most effective; or, as a Christmas wreath for the front door, a single, large one, decked instead in holly, ivy and ribbon bows, is more unusual and is easier to make, than the traditional ring shape.

Covered clothes-hangers are worth snapping up, even the most obviously home-sewn or knitted, for there is nothing like them for keeping in place clothes that would otherwise slip onto the wardrobe floor. If you find wooden coat-hangers for sale on the White Elephant stall, you might consider covering them yourself, using some of the beautiful silk, satin and velvet fabrics to be found in dresses or blouses on the Clothing stall. You will need wadding (from an old terylene-filled duvet or an anorak, perhaps) and a rectangle of pretty material, the narrow measurement of which should be enough to wrap around the wadded hanger plus an extra four centimetres for turnings, and the length of it must be a quarter again that of the hanger. This last is because the material is to be gathered, and it is the gathers that will grip the shoulders of the garment and keep them from sliding off; it also means that you don't have to fit the material precisely to the curved shape of the wood. Simply trim your rectangle of cloth into an oblong, press a turning of one and a half centimetres all around and sew continuous running stitches just half a centimetre from the edge. Place the wadded hanger in the middle and evenly draw up the material around it so that you have a narrow double frill along the top edge; stitch the two sides together along the line of your running stitches.

There are various refinements you can add to turn the hanger into a very attractive gift, and you may first like to see how the professionals do it; look at the hangers for sale in expensive lingerie shops and stores that specialise in lacy, feminine gifts. The first thought that will strike you is the amount of money they cost, the second that such an article *has* to be hand-made (hence the high price) and the shop's version is no better than anything you can make. To achieve a similar, luxurious finish cover the hook of the hanger with fine ribbon and add lace, either as a rosette or a frill in the centre, or inserted between the two sides as you bring them together to sew along the top (if the lace has been recycled from another jumble purchase, starch it first). Make a matching lace-trimmed bag for pot-pourri and hang it from the hook by a loop of ribbon; decorate with bows and artificial flowers.

If you sew a pair of hangers and scented bags as a gift, then attach them with shirring elastic to a piece of foil-covered card that fits the base of an attractive, lidded cardboard box, and no one will guess you didn't buy the set from the best shop in town – the trick being that the four pieces can be arranged to make the best use of the box, whatever its shape. If you have time, cover the container and base card alike with pretty wrapping paper, or, for an extra-special gift, with the same material as the covered hangers. You could lightly pad the sides, base and lid using left-over wadding and decorate the top of the box with the same lace; even attach another tiny pot-pourri sachet inside for added thoughtfulness. And how about producing a set of pin-striped hangers in a matching box as a gift for a gentleman? If you use an old suit for this, choose one of 'summer' weight to cut down on bulk and give a finer finish.

As the ideas begin to flow, your inventiveness will know no bounds. Most of the garments on the Clothing stall, by virtue of the very fact that they are constructed from fairly small pieces of material in the first place, will suggest revamping into quite tiny objects; unless, that is, you take up patchwork quilting on a huge scale or adopt Avril's idea – she's collecting as many printed Indian cotton wrap-around skirts as she can, to sew together in a parachute shape to 'tent' the ceiling of a room.

For you, the tiny objects you sew *could* be satin bikinis and velvet G-strings; but interest in making such things may soon begin to pall (unless, of course, you have built up a mail-order business selling sexy fripperies!). You could make beautifully hemmed silk handkerchiefs, a most genteel occupation, but boring before you've reached the fourth side of the first hanky; or you may begin to think of small gifts and decorations, quick to make and each one different, just to rivet the attention. Once again, a survey of stores in your nearest town will give you an inkling of the existing range (which you can immediately improve upon), quality and presentation. It will hearten you to think that your efforts will not look out of place amongst those bought from the most exclusive end of the market. And they will be consistently of that standard if you abide by a few simple rules – rules which ensure that your gifts are seen as 'hand-made' rather than 'home-made', a term only complimentary when applied to food.

Rule one is *never* use pinking shears. That toothed edge to the material is an immediate give-away of an unprofessional approach and can even be detected through a layer of fabric. Rule two: every time you sew a seam trim its raw edges, snip around curves to ease them and cut across corners as near to the stitching as you dare; this will stop bulky seams ruining the line. Rule three: press the article after every stage. Rule four: finish off all loose ends. Rule five: never leave a raw edge showing – mask it somehow, even if you only glue ribbon or braid along it. After that, everything depends on presentation, and if you find you enjoy making pretty little gifts you must keep on the look-out – not just for the few days before the gift has to be presented, but all year round – for fine-quality, well made containers of all kinds. Boxes with clear acetate lids are particularly good for showing off the contents, and wooden cigar boxes with hinged lids can look most impressive when covered. Pretty tea caddies can be given as a joke, containing something hand-sewn that is definitely not tea; and small baskets, once lined and decorated, can become, not just containers, but gifts in their own right. Storage of boxes need not be too difficult as many of them will fit one inside the other.

And it is not just boxes that should be thought of all year round. There is a natural tendency to dismiss an object or garment because it is out of season; Christmas baubles are slow to sell in January, but that's just when the householder who has decided to buy new ones next time will give the old ones to the jumble collectors. Likewise, a sundress that a jumbler would do battle for over the trestles in June will be cast aside with a shiver at an October sale.

Lateral thinkers who make their own gifts will not be so short-sighted. A sunny yellow silk shirt (with a frayed collar and torn buttonhole) found in November may remind you of Easter; good enough reason to buy and store it – the brainwave will come nearer the event. A springtime purchase of red satin may prompt a vision of plump shiny hearts hung on the Christmas tree or . . .

just a minute, isn't it Aunt Freda and Uncle Bill's ruby wedding anniversary soon? And how about another heart, attached by a safety pin to a Valentine's day card? Might be nice to give to a sweetheart; and a smaller heart, also on a pin, or a slide, or a haircomb, can be attached to a present instead of one of those inevitable, boring stick-on bows, making an extra little gift out of the decoration. And the red of the heart would go beautifully with this black silk scarf, bought over the trestle for a mere fivepence. How dramatic to wrap it round a present instead of more expensive paper, and so easy, for it will take the shape of any object however ungainly; all you have to do is tie the ends together and pin the heart on . . . or bunch the ends and bind them round with this white rope belt with the knotted ends, very masculine and sophisticated.

Visions of heaps of brightly coloured clothing and scarves scattered around your home, obscuring every surface as they await your treatment, can be dispelled if you are prepared to deal in a certain way with each item as you get it home to make it easier to store. If it is washable, then wash and iron it as it is, a complete garment. After that, with a ruthless eye, take the article 'off the bone': fillet it. You will never want to use material that has already been sewn into a seam as it will be needle-marked and a slightly different colour; neither will you want to keep any damaged or stained portions of material, as you will jeopardise the professional look of your finished article. Cut them out. Cut off the hem then cut away the good material from the side seam, around the armholes and the shoulders; abandon button and buttonhole strips

*'She takes jumble sales very seriously . . .'*

(but always keep good buttons) and cast off collars without a care – all you want to finish up with are flat and perfect pieces of material. Don't be tempted to unpick a bust dart so that you can keep the front in one piece, for the ghost of the stitching will always show in a certain light, however you wash and iron the cloth. The end result of the filleting operation will take up surprisingly little room and you will know then exactly how much material you have to play with.

Along with the fabric, you will need to store your constantly added-to collection of trimmings. Buttons, particularly heart or flower shapes and those with imitation gems set in, are very useful decorations and should be searched for at every jumble sale, as should old brooches, beads and sequins. Lace, ribbons and braids should be detached from the original garment, laundered and wound onto the cardboard tube from a tin foil roll.

Then, with the knowledge that you have the materials at hand to cope with any sudden whim, you can approach each celebration with a free and inventive spirit. A new baby in the family? Make a special card for the parents. Paint onto a piece of silk or satin a suitable motif (keep it simple, use pale watercolours or food dye and attempt to achieve an impression rather than a detailed picture), place a square of wadding behind and stitch through both layers to quilt the picture, or put a piece of plain material behind, stitch around the motif then pad it through a small hole cut in the backing. Cut out a frame from thin card to mount your picture, or better still, have handy a selection of three-fold cards, the middle fold having a square or oval shape removed through which you display your art and needlework. These can be bought ready cut and folded from craft shops. Alternatively, you will find suppliers of them, and other means for displaying your work, advertised in the back of craft and needlework magazines; try Audrey Babington's *Workbox*, a biannual publication that might give you some excellent ideas for things to make and how best to display them (ceramic pots, the lids of which are specifically made to contain miniature patchwork, for instance). But back to the new baby. You could make for it a soft and pretty segmented ball, or a white heart to hang by a ribbon in the pram; be sure to use approved toy filler for these, and for stuffed Christmas decorations (look back at Chapter Seven, page 53). The heart, white satin dripping with crystal beads and tiny bows with artificial flowers sewn onto the ends, could also be presented to a bride – presumably the new mother's younger sister! Or make the heart larger and decorate it with lace for a boudoir cushion; or make it as a pyjama case; or . . . but, hang on. There are lots of other shapes and dozens of other articles – for instance. . . . No, all that can be left to your own imagination. In the meantime, happy jumbling and may your brainwaves flow freely around the S-bend of your mind.

# APPENDIX

## For Those Interested; a History

In the beginning was the anthropoid who coveted his neighbour's stone axe. He acquired it, probably by foul means as barter had yet to be invented, and so was born the second-hand item.

Then came the market place, where craftsmen and peasants crouched in all weathers beside their meagre goods, laid out in the dust or mud, until a bright individual placed a board on two supports and invented the stall.

Not a lot happened to shopping for centuries after that. In the Middle Ages the population remained small and consisted in very unequal proportions of rich and poor, landowner and landworker; but most attended – or were represented at – the local weekly market (sometimes half a day's journey away) to sell their surplus produce and buy the things they couldn't make or grow for themselves.

The main concerns of the poor majority were to fill their tummies and to keep warm; and what income was left from the former was usually spent in pursuit of the latter, on second-hand clothing and footwear. Only the very rich heeded fashion's whim, and clothing for peasants was necessarily plain, simple and long-lasting; if it were to be brand new the wool must be spun and woven, or precious pennies given for a length of linen, and many painstaking hours spent with needle and thread in the poor light of a tallow candle after all the daylight had been spent on more important chores. Lives were short and the cloth tough, so garments would be willed from father to son to grandson, and if there was no male heir, or extreme poverty struck, would be sold to the 'phelipers' or 'fripperers' – dealers in old clothes. Many of the garments that found their way into the phelipers' clutches had been stolen, and complete outfits were taken off hanged men and women before rigor set in; but this held no horror for the purchaser, who might only earn tuppence a day as a common labourer when fine wool cloth cost three to five shillings a yard. As for household goods, metal was expensive (a brass jug would cost around seven shillings) so the cheaper alternatives of wooden trenchers and leather 'blackjack' drinking vessels were more often used, with pewter for those who could afford a little more. But there was no substitute for iron knives or cooking-pots, and the second-hand tradition is as firmly rooted in these goods as it is in clothing.

In the Middle Ages every town – generally smaller than a modern English village – had at least one mercer, or retail tradesman, whose ground-floor rooms would be filled with anything that could be picked up cheaply at the annual fairs. He made a poor living, for, at a time when bargains were traditionally struck between producer and purchaser in the open market, there was a great dislike of the middle-man, and a great distrust of his dark and smelly stock rooms where it was hard to see the quality of the goods on sale.

However, a massive upsurge in the population of London, unmatched elsewhere in the country, prompted the spread of shops. In the century up to 1640 the number of inhabitants rose from 60,000 to 300,000 or 400,000, of whom a growing but still small proportion were rich and would buy all sorts of items as fast as they could be manufactured; but the massive majority remained poor and were employed in the workshops that produced the goods.

To cater for all classes, pawnbrokers (first heard of towards the end of the fifteenth century) began to flourish, especially in London where the lower classes patronised Houndsditch, Long Lane and, later, Monmouth Street and Rosemary Lane – better known as Rag Fair – while the upper class, perhaps to finance a weekend at the races whilst temporarily out of funds, popped the family silver at more genteel establishments in Holywell Street. Some pawnbrokers became notorious for their activities and many were the stories of interest rates at eighty per cent, with instant forfeit of goods if a payment was missed. But this was not the brokers' only way of acquiring stock, for like the phelipers before them they would buy from the hangman or the heirs of the more peacefully deceased, from people in desperately reduced circumstances, from jailors selling (for commission) the belongings of an inmate to gain the price of release or a meal, and from thieves who would fish, with rod and line, for the good or fancy clothes of anyone foolish enough to leave a casement window open at night. The merchants prospered and grew fat, even at the height of the plague, when it would seem that the only objection to their disease-infested trade was to their practice of hanging clothes outside where they might blow in the faces of passers-by.

Many of the so-called shops in London were really sheds or 'bulks' leaning against sturdier walls; some of them were no more than a seat and a roof held up by posts. Others were roofed-over stalls with roughly planked sides and the board hinged up to block the window at night, and down in the morning to form the counter on which the stock was displayed and over which deals were struck. This style of trading lasted well into the eighteenth century and the phrase for starting and finishing the day's business long remained 'to open and close the window'.

During the eighteenth century the working classes in the south of England relied almost entirely on second-hand clothes (although servants' livery was still part of their wages) whilst northern farm labourers still preferred to spin, weave and sew their own. But north and south alike wore hard-wearing wool and linen, the efficient laundering of which varied less according to regional differences than to circumstances and determination, often against almost insuperable odds. From the start house-wives saw the wisdom of taking the laundry to the water supply – the river – where they 'beetled' it on the rocks or trampled it in large wooden tubs, often ending up with legs grossly swollen and mottled black and blue from the icy waters. But as the towns grew and slums abounded, tightly packed onto the smallest pieces of land (each house so full that sometimes three families shared a single room), the river was replaced by a pump sometimes a mile away. Just fetching enough water for the family's daily needs meant a walk in all weathers carrying heavy pots or buckets, a tedious wait for a turn at the spout and a struggle back home with the extra weight of often foul and brackish water. It is no wonder that worn-out or sluttish souls gave up the battle for personal hygiene. As Chas. Hindley commented: 'A Whitechapel beau is one who dresses with a needle and thread and undresses with a knive', while Thomas Turner, a Sussex grocer of the 1750s, was of the opinion that, 'A bath should be taken every spring, along with the annual blood letting.'

The government hardly helped matters when, for two centuries from 1643, it heavily taxed soap, so those fastidious and resourceful souls amongst the poor turned to stale urine, or dung steeped in cold water, as bleaching agents. To dissolve grease they produced lye, which was laboriously made by allowing water to drip slowly through wood ash. This was all very well for keeping linen shifts presentable, but there was little that could be done to remove the grime and fleas from a double-quilted horse-hair petticoat, or the grease and bad smells from a pair of leather stays. And who would be so foolish as to dunk her heavy stuff (wool) gown in water, where it might shrink, when she would have to shiver in her underwear until it dried?

Life and the second-hand trade seemed set to continue in just the same way for ever, but then came the Industrial Revolution. What started as a tiny, shifting pebble of progress in the textile industry soon became a massive landslide that crushed the working classes in its path. Looking back on the achievements, both agricultural and industrial, from 1760 onwards, it would seem to have been a thrilling, breathtaking time of golden opportunity, full of magical inventions and discoveries. In reality there was chronic unemployment as skilled men were displaced by each new machine which could be run by women and children for a pittance. And the man who turned to crime to feed his family could expect deportation or the hangman's noose if caught, while the dealers and pawnbrokers who gave him scant pennies for what he stole grew fat and smug in the knowledge that the law could not touch them. At one time there were thought to be more than three thousand 'receivers' openly selling stolen goods in London alone.

The misery continued as redundant farm labourers and their families poured into towns to look for work, while the paths of the massive new steam locomotives were taken straight through the already overcrowded slum areas, making thousands homeless or worse – eligible for the workhouse, the madhouse, or the paupers' grave. But as the rookeries and stews crashed down before the railway's might they took with them a legacy of over-crowded, insanitary conditions, crumbling brickwork and earth floors, signalling the start of an immense housing boom. Six million homes were built in Victoria's reign, many of them in new suburbs only made possible by the rail links to the centre of towns. And most of the new houses were scaled-down versions of better-class dwellings. If a young man was intelligent, ambitious and had received some schooling he could become a clerk (for there was no lack of paperwork in the boom days) and rent one of these tiny terraced palaces in a wide and leafy street away from town. His wife would find she had a parlour to keep for Sunday visitors, a range instead of an open fire on which to cook, and running water from a tap in the scullery, while in the yard or garden was a lavatory that was all their very own.

They were part of the new middle class, a rôle they took very seriously, strictly by the book of etiquette, for few had been brought up to have an easy familiarity with good manners; and suddenly for them to buy anything second-hand was a great *faux pas*. As they worked hard at being nicer and more proper than the next couple, the threat to a reputation should a dress be recognised as having had a previous life on someone else's back was worse than the threat to the purse posed by buying new.

Now the tallyman's star was rising. He had long been thought of as even more of a rogue than the pawnbroker for his new but shoddy goods, high interest rates and sleight of hand with the 'tally' – a stick, split down the middle, half of which was kept by the trader and half by the illiterate customer; when a payment was made the two halves were put together and a mark made across both; when the bill was paid both pieces were broken. His reputation was not soon to improve, but his goods became more sought-after. Although the poor were forced to make as much use as ever of the pawnbrokers and dealers, the credit shops and travelling 'Scotch drapers' with their tawdry goods, they couldn't fail to be aware of the upwardly spiralling consumerism, often shown to best advantage by the chain stores and department stores that now sprang up in every high street, openly flaunting their desirable wares.

Mass production, made possible in the late 1860s by inventions such as sewing, knitting and shoe-making machines, meant that these wonderful new emporia were full of reasonably priced copies of exclusive models. For the first time, fashion was being urged upon the man and woman in the street – literally, as the new, huge plate-glass shop windows showed tempting displays of everything from buttons to beds, with banners proclaiming them 'the latest thing' and 'direct from Paris'.

Gradually more and more people found they could afford to live well, and women who had been brought up to hard work became ladies of leisure. Maids were hired, or labour-saving gadgets took away the drudgery of housework. Some thought themselves in heaven, but many chafed at their inactivity and engaged in the only honourable occupation allowed in the middle-class code – Good Works. Those involved in poor relief might be required to collect and distribute good-quality second-hand clothes, and often a scheme was used whereby the church-wardens of the parish, having deliberated at length on a supplicant's extreme poverty and good character, would graciously bestow on him a ticket allowing him to purchase, for a minimal sum, a pair of trousers for himself or boots for his child. This scheme had first been employed three hundred years earlier when the price of corn soared out of reach of the poor; but in those days they took their tickets to the mill to collect a pan or sack of flour. Now they were more likely to attend the church or church hall, where clothes would be laid out on trestle tables with kindly ladies to dispense them.

The ticket system resurfaced during the Second World War as an ideal way of ensuring that those familes who emerged from the ruins of their homes could be shod and clad from the small pool of new and second-hand garments kept by the WVS, the Salvation Army and others, but the trestle table format has become the jumble sale of today and has moved on from being a preserve of the poor to achieve the status of a respectable hobby. It was not an easy transformation. Second-hand clothes in the past were more likely than not to be jumping with lice and fleas and full of stains, or even disintegrating from the action of sweat at the armholes, which was all very well when the clothes of everyone, rich or poor, were in that condition. But during the twentieth century insect vermin have been controlled (DDT was invented in 1939), most houses have a good supply of hot water, while detergents and stain removers have become increasingly sophisticated, and deodorants and anti-perspirants mean that the underarms of clothing are now rarely rotted or discoloured.

The first of the man-made fabrics, rayon, went into general production in the 1890s and was soon freely available, making women's clothing, at least, cheaper and more plentiful; even before the First World War clothes merely needed to look dated rather than worn out before they were discarded. But, although the condition of the second-hand garments for sale improved, more and more people found distasteful the whole idea of wearing others' cast-offs – or, for that matter, using other people's books, sheets, kitchen tools, cutlery, pans and anything else now found at a jumble sale.

This attitude was due in part to a better understanding of the causes of disease, for although Charles Wesley had long before preached that 'cleanliness is next to godliness' it took Florence Nightingale as recently as the Crimean War of 1854–6, to show that strict hygiene kept people alive and that germs could be passed on by touch. At a time when it was normal for children to die of what are now considered trivial ailments, the better mother was one who took care not to allow possibly contaminated items into her home. It is hard to believe that penicillin was only introduced during the Second World War and although it miraculously brought down the death rate from most infectious diseases, it took a long while for the population to take its life-saving qualities for granted, especially as there was currently an epidemic it couldn't control – poliomyelitis!

Mercifully, the Salk and Sabin vaccines of the mid 1950s stopped the spread of this crippling disease and gradually people forgot their fears, but they didn't return immediately to second-hand shopping, for these were the years of the new world, when jobs, money and goods were plentiful and all the ravages and restraints of the war were reversed.

To the children of the 1950s everything was new: the

houses that grew out of the bomb-sites all around them, the complete New Towns that rose, fresh and modern, called 'Stevenage', 'Harlow' and 'Croydon'. They were impressed by the 'Festival of Britain', a euphoric, if optimistic, celebration of all the magnificent new products that could be manufactured in this country. They saw the old, brown, war-time 'utility' furniture in their living rooms replaced by 'contemporary' G-Plan or Ercol, folk-weave-covered studio couches and pale beechwood chairs with spindly, splayed legs, and the cold lino and rag rugs on which they played changed for fitted carpets, all on hire-purchase – the never-never.

Mother was no longer expected to slave over a boiler and mangle, with wash-board, scrubbing brush and red-raw hands, but was bought by father a gleaming new washing machine – no doubt under the influence of magazine advertisements that showed attractive, prosperous families living in harmony amongst their many possessions. The illusion was furthered by television portrayals of the American way of life: prettier, richer families with wider smiles and curious electrical gadgets called 'blenders' and 'juicers'. In 1953 anybody who was anybody bought or rented a television on which to watch the Coronation of Queen Elizabeth, and few sets were returned to the shops afterwards; though radio still had its loyal listeners and millions of people were totally involved in the middle-class lives of the Archers and the Dales.

And the children grew into a new breed called 'teenagers' who had complete industries dedicated to their needs. Yet they found it all smacked of being moulded to fit their parents' cosy but boring lives, and many of them began looking for something different, something to shock.

They found Oxfam – and the Jumble Sale.

In their eyes the clothes looked more interesting than the crimplene mini skirts and nylon polo-neck jumpers currently flooding the new boutiques, while jumble sale purchases had the twin advantages of costing very little and thoroughly discomfiting parents who had spent their lives trying desperately never to have to buy second-hand goods again. It was great fun to unearth something last worn in the 1920s by a flapper, or an Edwardian gentleman's richly embroidered waistcoat, whilst the acquisition of a long fur coat brought far more prestige in some circles than a brand-new, shop-bought Mary Quant mini plastic mac – even with matching silver plastic boots!

If they enjoyed shocking their parents, it was a different matter with their peers, amongst whom it was important to look like one of the group; but even so, most of them found a use for second-hand clothes. Motor-bike-loving 'Rockers' of both sexes liked their denim jeans and leather jackets 'broken in' for them – both were uncomfortable when stiff and new – and the recognised treatment for new jeans was to wear them in the bath and let them dry on the body, shrinking to a skin-tight fit. If this could be achieved without hours of discomfort and risk of pneumonia, a nicely worn garment could be forgiven its faded patches, which soon became so much the norm that those who bought new went to extreme lengths to age the garment artificially.

A totally different style was adopted by the 'Mods', who were far more vain and very concerned about the clothes they wore, the boys trying for the look of the Regency Buck (the richer-quality garments to be found at jumble sales suited them very well). Lace frills and embroideries that would attract attention at auction much later in the century could be picked up for pennies in the 1960s, and various entrepreneurs, feeling innovative no doubt, opened trendy boutiques selling fusty old uniforms with lots of gold braid and dress shirts of a much earlier era. Many a young blade swaggered down fashionable King's Road in London wearing an ancient frock-coat, or tight Edwardian striped trousers bought from such establishments. Soon the rag trade followed on and began making clothes in a style to suit and eventually these boutiques went out of fashion.

The third style was 'Hippy', featuring what are now called 'ethnic' clothes. This meant that the girls bought anything made of cotton, linen or wool second-hand, especially if it was long and floating. The boys favoured collarless shirts, any amount of which could be found on the trestles, and as the genuine Hippy rarely earned any money, being dedicated to peace, love and flower-power for all hours of the day, the low cost of the transaction was a great advantage. Needless to say, the manufacturers didn't try to court this trade quite so assiduously.

By the 1970s the young people were becoming parents themselves, as staid and stereotyped as those against whom they had rebelled, but they still saw nothing demeaning about buying second-hand clothes and were grateful for anything that reduced demands on the family purse; inflation was biting hard. Baby clothes were then, and still are, some of the best bargains to be found at a jumble sale, very often hardly worn at all and retaining a lot of charm even when tumbled together in an untidy mass. Any squeamishness is soon overridden by hard-headed practicality. And even if the Thatcher years brought prosperity, the lure of the jumble sale and the excitement of the unknown bargain waiting on the other side of the hall door still proves irresistible, while the delight in snaffling a beautifully cut Pierre Cardin blazer in excellent condition from a pile of 1970s polyester, wide-lapel outcasts before others realise its presence, is as heady a feeling as having bet on a winning horse. If the good person behind the trestle looks at it with some surprise (and, perhaps, envy that she didn't spot it first), purses her lips and says, 'That's rather a good jacket', causing a trembling anticipation of the high price she will ask for it, his or her subsequent 'I'll have to ask for twenty-five pence' is like handing the winning ticket to the bookie and watching him shell out – for that blazer in the shop is worth around £145, not a bad return on a twenty-five pence stake!

Of course, the excitement of what might be waiting on the trestle table and a down-to-earth attitude to life has kept, for the jumble sale, many loyal fans who ignored the snooty comments of others during the unfashionable years and now survive to be the indomitable types at the head of the queue. They are usually well dressed (but not so well that the jumble sale helpers charge them an inflated price) and often well spoken; that lady at the front might be the wife of a consultant surgeon, and her friend that of the area bank manager. They can tell a Royal Doulton plate at fifty paces and a cashmere sweater by touch alone, like to choose only Gucci and Jaeger labels for themselves and take home Next and St Michael items for the cleaning lady.

At a jumble sale now there is an almost infinite choice in both variety and quality, for it is often used as a dumping ground by many women who virtuously give away clothes they have tired of so they can complain that they have nothing to wear and thus justify refilling their wardrobes; they can't imagine how anyone could bear to miss the joys of an expensive shopping spree in town. As long as such people exist, so will the jumble sale – *vive la différence*!

# Index